A

BETWEEN FRIENDS

Also by Jeannette Ferrary
(with Louise Fiszer)

California-American Cookbook:
Innovations on American Regional Dishes

Season to Taste:
Herbs and Spices in American Cooking

Between

Friends

M. F. K. Fisher
and Me

Jeannette Ferrary

THE ATLANTIC MONTHLY PRESS
NEW YORK

For my parents,
Loretta and Fred Ferrary

Portions of this book appeared, in somewhat different form, in The New York Times, The New York Times Book Review, *and* The Journal of Gastronomy.

Published simultaneously in Canada
Printed in the United States of America
First Edition

Library of Congress Cataloging-in-Publication Data

Ferrary, Jeannette, 1941–
    Between friends: M. F. K. Fisher and me / Jeannette Ferrary
    ISBN 0-87113-450-0
    1. Fisher, M. F. K. (Mary Frances Kennedy), 1908– . 2. Food writers—United States—Biography. I. Title.
    TX649.F5F47   1991   641'.092—dc20   90-23591

Design by Mentyka/Schlott Design

The Atlantic Monthly Press
19 Union Square West
New York, NY 10003

First printing

Acknowledgments

As usual, I can think of no way to thank Peter Carroll enough, at least on paper, for the endlessness of his enthusiasm and encouragement. Although I often hesitated to ask him to read something over one more time, he never hesitated to offer. He is one of those rare people who can be brilliant and listen at the same time, doing both with equal intensity. What can I say? How about I make dinner tonight?

I am grateful, as well, to the several people so important in M. F. K. Fisher's life that only they could have supplied the details and context, the color and perspective, I would have known in no other way. For the hours they generously spent with me, remembering, answering and especially asking, I thank Marsha Moran, M. F. K. Fisher's long-time assistant; I thank Judith Jones who unstintingly opened her memories to me and whose gentle confusion about my intentions for this book helped clarify them in my own mind; I thank Bob Lescher who, when I met him, brought me coffee in a cup shaped like a miniature chamber pot, which broke the ice, so to speak, and began a warm all-afternoon chat that has never really stopped; I thank

Eleanor Friede for hours of beautiful reminiscences and honest reevaluations and lunch, at which everything not only tasted good but meant something; I thank Norah Barr for almost eighty years of background and memorabilia, and for making me feel welcome as family.

I am glad that Fred Hill, my friend and agent, always knows what to do and when and to whom, all of which is his particular genius, but I thank him most of all for caring about everything so much.

As for John Barstow, my editor, I am fortunate that while this book was under his aegis, he had nothing else to do but read its every jot and tittle, no other project in need of his wit and insight and elegance of style, no concern beyond the welfare of these pages, no phone calls to make but the ones to me and none to answer but mine, any time of the day or night. At least he made it seem that way. All his other authors, I know, feel likewise.

For various kindnesses I thank Connie Goldman, *New York Times* editor Margot Slade, and filmmaker Barbara Wornum. I am very grateful to Ed Kleinschmidt, a great poet, who has better things to do than help laser-print people's manuscripts but who did it anyway.

And finally, I thank my daughter, Natasha, now ten, for waiting just another minute, just to the end of the paragraph, about a hundred million times.

I do not know which to prefer,
The beauty of inflections
Or the beauty of innuendos,
The blackbird whistling
Or just after.

——from "Thirteen Ways of
Looking at
a Blackbird"
by Wallace Stevens

Contents

Preface

Sometime in 1977 I found myself fascinated, for the second time, with M. F. K. Fisher's *The Art of Eating*. Almost immediately I wrote a letter to the author, but I had no idea where to send it. It wasn't an important letter; it just said how much I loved her writing, all of it, every last scrap that I had thus far come across. Because the book had been published by Alfred A. Knopf, I sent my letter to New York, hoping they had someone employed in those hallowed halls who would send it on to her, wherever she was.

Soon afterward I received a reply from Mrs. Fisher herself, who, to my amazement and in testimony to my ignorance, lived not far from me, in Glen Ellen, California. After a short period of correspondence, she invited me for lunch. Needless to say, I drove up as soon as I could, not knowing what to expect. Now, over a decade later, I have made the two-hour journey to Glen Ellen countless times; and once, in her more agile days, she traveled down to my home. Over this period much has happened and continues to happen in her career and in her life. But one thing stays the same: I never know what to expect.

Other people feel likewise.

Up there with her time lasts longer. She puts on the round wooden table a bowl of roasted red peppers (and one yellow one, because she never stops when things are merely perfect). These peppers, plump and sensuous as Rubens's ladies' thighs, smell of coriander and fire and olives. As we eat, the air between us becomes an invisible brocade of stories and twice-told tales, of allegories, moral and otherwise, of chatter and not exactly gossip, but close. I have tried, on several occasions, to capture these moments, to bring them back alive.

Whenever I've written about her, I've sent her my stories in fear and trepidation. "Try to read this and not get mad at the same time," I once said. I've always been a little afraid because in my stories she is the way she is. Her reactions, as I might have suspected, are never what I might have suspected. In fact, she has told me a few times that I am the only one who writes about her as if she were a real person. ("I get so tired of reading about that sweet, dear lady smiling away" she once confided). But I have never written about her *for* anything. I have written about her the way one writes a poem and for the same reason: because I felt like it, or because I needed to, or because I loved her a bit more urgently than usual at that moment.

The last time I gave her something I'd written, she lost it. I was waiting for a reply, a reaction, and when I didn't get one, I thought this time she was angry about some of the "honestisms" in the piece. But when I mentioned it, she looked genuinely puzzled and then terribly embarrassed that the piece had apparently disappeared. I gave her another copy. Shortly thereafter we were speaking by phone, verbally searching our calendars for a mutually free date, when she said, "Oh, by the way, I read the story you left, about the books? I loved it; really, dear, I did." And then she said—and this is the point of all this—"I wish you were writing my life."

I have spent afternoons with her in Glen Ellen while people in the background have been riffling through her books and bookshelves, writing down years and locations of the various editions of her books, recording facts, chronologies, events. These are not my methods. For me they haven't much to do with who she is, what she believes, what she does and tries to do, how she affects the universe, why people love her. So I have written about her life this way, the way I know her and the way I know how.

Because Mrs. Fisher has written so often of her own life, any book about her must take an unusual form. Essentially this memoir is like a collection of personal snapshots, mixing current event and flashback in order to build, chapter by chapter, a composite picture of M. F. K. Fisher. Although the stories take place in the present, they concern events throughout her life—past, present, and semi-imaginary—that she has openly shared with me or simply grumbled about in my presence. As you proceed through each succeeding chapter, I hope you will come to know M. F. K. Fisher as a person, reaching, by the book's end, an understanding of who she is, what she represents, what place she fills—in short, why she has fascinated, frustrated, angered, delighted, and befuddled so many people for so long.

This memoir is a collection of appreciations, not her biography in any formal sense, but her life, as I've experienced it.

———————————

An Invitation from
M. F. K. Fisher:

Why Me?

Because I keep a diary, I know what M. F. K. Fisher was doing on the morning of October 3, 1977. My entry for that date reads, "Went to MFK's for lunch and luckily (considering her reaction) desisted from bringing pumpkins ('Who needs them?') and croissants ('I don't eat that sort of thing anymore')."

In other words, on that fateful October morn M. F. K. Fisher was at her home in Glen Ellen making lunch for me and my friend Frances. By some quirk that I couldn't fathom (though I had my pet theory about the matter), she had invited the two of us to lunch. While she waited for us to drive the two hours from south of San Francisco to her place, she had plenty of time to prepare the wondrous things she would serve us. We knew already they would be wondrous, whatever they might be, because of who was making them. M. F. K. Fisher preparing lunch for us (it didn't make sense): two mere fans whose only apparent qualification to be luncheon guests was that we had read all her books (unless you count my theory, which had to do with the cooking school Frances and I were planning to attend in the south of France).

Of course, she could have invited me up out of simple curiosity. I had been writing to Mary Frances with some regularity for over a year, ever since I discovered that she lived less than two hours from me in California. Before that I'd thought she'd be living in exotic places or in no place in particular, floating on ocean liners, walking along piers, considering oysters, making careful, clean drawings with her fine-line words. The first time I wrote to her was out of pure, uncontrollable enthusiasm undiminished by my ignorance of how one reaches the authors of books. This naive combination must have had its appeal, because one otherwise ordinary day the mailman topped off a pile of the usual postal irrelevancies with a white business envelope. The name and address of M. F. K. Fisher blared out from the left-hand corner in tiny print, finished off with a zip code not all that different from my own. This was the first time I'd had one of these experiences—so it seemed particularly important—in which someone admired or famous suddenly becomes real. A bit too real, as it usually turns out, and ultimately disappointing more often than not. Hardly anybody is what they're cracked up to be. But the first time it happens seems like a miracle, with its own unspeakable larger-than-life-ness.

"It's probably just a form letter," I said to Frank, the maddeningly uncurious mailman, my voice cracking with self-conscious anticipation. I didn't want him to think that I actually knew M. F. K. Fisher or that I was going to be expecting any special postal consideration from then on.

He just smiled at me as usual and said, cryptically but not unkindly, "Most things are."

It wasn't a form letter. It was an answer to my questions, a thank-you for my words of appreciation, even a few inquiries about my own interests. For the next week, off and on, I answered that letter. I wanted it to be short, nonchalant, and chatty, even if I had to use up a pad and a half of yellow lined paper to get it right. When it was done (finally), I ran out to the mail truck to hand my letter to Frank, who couldn't have missed the gleam in my eye as I said, "It wasn't a form letter."

"Oh, good," he replied, making me think that mailmen might have some feeling of pride in delivering real letters, correspondence between real citizens, such as their mailmen forefathers had delivered before them, and their forefathers, and so on back to the pony express or whoever did it.

"Have you ever read her stuff?" I asked, emboldened by my realization of our mutual sensibilities.

"Whose stuff?" he asked, with a look of confusion that was clearly a plea for some explanation. It was at that moment I first realized that some people had not heard of M. F. K. Fisher. I had recently rediscovered her books and considered them classics in their genre or maybe even a genre in themselves. And since I thought them classics, I assumed that everyone else was familiar with them and had read them years ago. But with Fisher, either people don't know her work at all, or they've read every last tingling word they can find and will worship her forever for her insights and understanding. Her readers relate to her work as if she's written it for them, selecting among her experiences those which resonate with their own. Then they sit down and "write back," telling her how her words helped them through the tragic hot-tub drowning of their cat, Mergatroyd, or brought back memories of old Aunt Minnie's *babka* that they always dreaded when they were kids but would give their right arm to taste one more time. ("Those are the kinds of letters I get," she once explained with a sigh, a contented sigh, I think.) Then she answers them, and they answer her, and the next thing she's inviting them for lunch if they live near enough to come, which Frances and I did.

"What should we bring her?" Frances asked ominously once the joy of accepting this unimaginable invitation had hit its height. In the aftermath of that joy it dawned on us that we should bring some food thing to her who knew everything about food, including what it means. We knew she loved France—she had once said, "I am more of me in France, more of the way I think I am. I'm more awake, more aware, and as far as senses and personality, stronger. Every minute is more of a minute there." So we decided she must love croissants, or at least think of them kindly and not too philosophically. We weren't very worried because, like many women in their thirties, we were just then getting quite interested in more advanced food ourselves. We thought we knew that sophisticated gourmets would never turn down a croissant or escargots or duck *à l'orange* or sweetbreads *à la mode de Caen* or mousse *au chocolat.* But the only practical choice seemed the croissants. Besides, I knew of a bakery, Pâtisserie Napoléon, run by a young French couple who made the biggest, golden-brownest, flakiest, butter-bound croissants in San Mateo County; plus you could get them warm from the oven if you got there first thing in the morning, which we resolved to do.

It was a beautifully bright-sun Monday when we started our long drive to Fisher's home in the Sonoma wine country. We had one short detour to make, one useless detour, it turned out: Pâtisserie Napoléon, like many bakeries, is closed on Mondays.

Frances and I looked at each other and laughed nervously.

Oh, never mind, we were sure to find something along the way. But though the route took us all through San Francisco, across the Golden Gate Bridge, along the blue-splashed curves of Sausalito and Marin County, we were mostly on freeways which offered few gourmet enticements that one could perceive at fifty-five miles per hour. We knew we were nearing Fisher's more rural territory when we started seeing signs that offered

MANURE. INQUIRE AT BARN.
SHEEPSKIN SEAT COVERS
REAL BEEF JERKY
WANTED CLEAN FILL. NO RUBBISH

We were getting desperate when we spotted the fruit and vegetable stand. It was one of those country markets spilling over with oranges and apples and too much zucchini from nearby farms. It didn't look as sophisticated as what we were hoping for, but it did look authentic. That might make up for it.

Once inside we were surprised to discover a large wine selection, a whole section of different kinds of packaged dried beans, and various brands of herb vinegars. We walked from one side to the other, increasingly amazed with each step.

"Hey, Frances," I called from the remarkably well-stocked canned foods, "do you remember what she said about canned *pâté de foies truffes* in *An Alphabet for Gourmets*?"

"No," she said, very excited over in the root-vegetable area, "but I do remember what she said about new potatoes in *How to Cook a Wolf*. She loves them!"

Our eyes lit up: great, great. Here they were, the little pink darlings, all smooth and newborn-looking. We found a paper sack and started to fill it with enthusiasm and potatoes. Then Frances said, "Do you really think it's appropriate to bring M. F. K. Fisher a sack of potatoes?"

Obviously we had adjusted too quickly to this rural context and its realm of homey possibilities. We dropped the potatoes and returned to the vinegars. The one with a gray, wilted-looking sprig stuck into a pile of small brown pebbles was called rosemary garlic and was out of the question. But there was another with a frilly bouquet waving from its center (lemon thyme) that didn't look bad. The minute we faced each other directly, however, we lost confidence. As we turned to leave, we fell into a pile of pumpkins that someone had set up as a display, this being the season. Although we were definitely cross as we pulled each other up and straightened our clothes, we had to admit that only one who is totally distracted or has no talent for peripheral vision could possibly have walked into this most conspicuous orange mountain.

The pumpkins came in every personality: the fat jollies with strong stems, the smooth, plump babies, the narrow-cheeked stern-uncle pumpkins that already looked like the frowning jack-o'-lanterns they would become.

We could bring her many pumpkins, a variety, or a bunch of the minis or one enormous pumpkin we could call the spirit o' Halloween as we handed it to her.

We'd better not hand it to her, we agreed: it might be too heavy. If we had any hesitation about this choice, it disappeared when we realized we could not lift the horrible orange monstrosity ourselves. We must be losing our minds altogether. Gift giving can do that to a person.

So we climbed back into the car and within fifteen minutes we were pulling into the driveway. It was the first of a hundred times to come that I would see the sign at the entrance: "TRESPASSERS WILL BE VIOLATED. NO ADMITTANCE. BOUVERIE RANCH PENAL CODE 602."

A rather belligerent welcome, I thought, knocking on the door, empty-handed except for the flowers Frances had picked from her garden.

"Come in," we heard in instant reply. And there she

was. She was smiling, that was the most important thing. She looked at us with gray-blue happy eyes, red ripe cheeks, arched eyebrows, and perfect teeth. Here she was sixty-nine years old, and she looked like a cross between Katharine Hepburn and any freckle-faced kid.

We walked in and automatically, as if this were the accustomed procedure, hugged each other.

"Oh, this must be . . . Jeannette? And this is . . . Frances. Oh, yes. Oh, I hope you didn't have a terrible drive. Such a long way."

That's the way she brought us in, into her house that pretty October noon, into her life, no questions asked.

"I was just fixing our lunch," she said, walking across the living room, with its womby wood-burning stove, and on into the kitchen. There was no real separation between the rooms: they just flowed in and out of each other, the way living and cooking are supposed to.

"How about a little white wine?" she asked, opening the refrigerator. The door had a shelf full of wines from which she picked a bottle she'd probably intended to serve, since it was already uncorked.

"I hope this is all right," she said, filling two wine glasses with the lemon-colored liquid and telling us it was made by some grape growing family that lived in Napa and how they got into the wine business and who their ancestors were and a few old scandals that kept the family together, so that by the time she gave me the wine glass, I felt as if I were holding a whole heritage in my hands. And it tasted more interesting than it otherwise would have, I'm sure.

What a good idea for a wine tasting, I thought: instead of some viticulturist or enologist telling everyone to notice the cherry nose or the chocolate finish, they could have M. F. K. Fisher or someone tell the family history, complete with any salacious rumors, past or present. I wanted to mention it to her (didn't she write quite a bit about wine over the years?), but I thought better of it. After all, we'd just met; maybe next time.

I think she gave us some nuts or something to eat, but we were so nervous, we just sat there, on the couch across from the fireplace, smiling like two fools.

"How do you two know each other?" she asked.

"Oh. Uh, . . . poetry," we said, actually mumbled, simultaneously, suddenly realizing that poetry, indeed, was how we knew each other.

"Poetry?" she repeated, a bright delight sounding in her voice, as if she were thankful we hadn't said, "bridge," or "tennis."

Heartened, I went on to explain how Frances and I had met when we were both asked to read our poetry at Stanford University on the occasion of International Women's Day Year or International Women's Year Day—I couldn't remember which at the moment. Soon we were chatting along about women in literature, including Colette, whom I knew she greatly admired. I had been trying to like Colette for some time, yawning my way through *The*

Ripening Seed and various translations of *Chéri*. But so far it was like reading science fiction or something: I just couldn't connect with her world. I had only myself to blame, I was sure, because I couldn't read her in the original. I tried to steer the conversation away from Colette. Since Frances is from the South, we burrowed deep into the works of Eudora Welty, who once had the same literary agent as Mary Frances.

"He was always sure she would be a success," she said. "A commercial success, I mean," she added, by which she seemed to mean number of sales. "But I don't care about that. Never did. I always write what I want to write."

She invited us to the table, a thick round of dark wood brightened with three yellow flowered napkins, three moss-green plates with little chips on the edges, a basket of rolls, and a salad bowl full of fat red and gold peppers steeped in unembarrassed quantities of olive oil and garlic.

"*Chermoula,*" she pronounced it and then, when no glint of recognition was forthcoming from either of us nouveau food sophisticates, "It's Moroccan, but I have the recipe from some funny old book I've had for years. A wonderful book, really."

She lifted the voluptuous reclining pepper strips onto our plates, and the air filled with their sweet yet sharp ambivalence. She served us a salad of delicate greens, chopped egg, and plump, pink prawns. How perfectly the croissants would have complemented this menu! Dare we mention it? Oh, yes, friendliness was growing in the air among us. We could say anything now.

"We wanted to bring you something today," I started, leading up to a description of the Pâtisserie Napoléon, with its ambitious young Parisians and their croissants.

"Croissants?" she echoed with a questioning tone. "I don't eat that sort of thing anymore."

Frances and I looked at each other, breathing unheard sighs of relief at our close call. For my part, I skipped the part of the story about how we couldn't get any croissants because the place was closed and went right on to the nice fruit and vegetable stand.

"They had millions of pumpkins," I began, tentatively.

"Pumpkins," she repeated. "Who needs them?"

No sense mentioning them now, I thought with a quick glance at Frances, who rolled her eyes in recognition of our second narrow escape. I was about to tell Mary Frances what else they had there when she went into a lengthy aside about these roadside markets and what a fraud they all are. They buy their produce, she explained, from the same places as the supermarkets and not from the small local growers. Then they try to look like a community farmers' market.

"Yes, that's terrible, dishonest, really," I said, clearing my throat, "but one thing they did have there were these herb vinegars. They looked quite pretty in their little bottles."

They may look pretty, she came right back, but they have no taste, and of course they charge much too much. "All it is," she explained, pointing vaguely out the window, "is some good wine vinegar and an herb that still has some life left in it." I followed her hand with my eyes and found it was pointing to the windowsill, on which were lined up three long-necked bottles. Inside each some frilly branches were drifting along, imparting life to their fluid surroundings.

"Oh, you make your own herb vinegars?" Frances asked rhetorically but so inaudibly that Mary Frances didn't hear anyway.

"Won't you have a little more?" Mary Frances asked during what she thought was the brief lull. By now Frances and I understood it was time to stop this conversation about what we didn't bring today while we were ahead. But Mary Frances was the one who changed the subject. And when she did so, I thought I detected a clue about why she had invited us there in the first place.

"Have you heard from Simone Beck?" she asked.

"Why, yes, we did. Just the other day. She must be back from Venice or wherever she was teaching. I think the place she wrote from is called Plascassier."

"Yes," Mary Frances nodded, dipping a crumb of her roll into the *chermoula*'s olive oil. "That's the place she and Julia have together near Grasse. You'll be staying there in the little house if you take that course with Simca."

Simca is Simone Beck's nickname, the name she used on *Simca's Cuisine,* the book that was responsible for stirring our interest in her cooking course. But she is more familiar to most people as the co-author, with Julia Child and Louisette Bertholle, of *Mastering the Art of French Cooking.* These three had started the cooking school called L'École des

Trois Gourmandes, headquartered in Grasse, in the south of France, on a big piece of land where the Childs and Becks lived at least part of the year.

"Well, unless something really earth shattering happens, we will be taking that course," Frances assured her. "I can hardly wait. I love that whole area, especially the French Riviera, don't you?"

She did indeed. She wished she could go there again herself, and she was certainly going to try.

"Soon, I hope," she said wistfully, her voice trailing off as if she knew, somehow, that she never would travel that far again. Did we know the works of Marcel Pagnol, she asked, especially his three comedies, *Marius, Fanny,* and *César,* set in Marseille? And next we were talking of van Gogh in Arles and how he, too, was inspired by that magical area. Across the newly placed plate of shortbread cookies, Frances and I stole some more of the meaningful glances by which we seemed to be communicating this afternoon. This was not at all what we had expected, we agreed with our eyes.

Certainly it was true that Mary Frances had invited me to lunch shortly after I wrote her that I was going to Grasse with my friend Frances to take a cooking course with Simone Beck. It was as if I had declared my intentions, become certified. If I were this serious about food and the knowledge thereof, then I qualified for what many referred to as an audience with her, my friend Frances thrown into the bargain. That was my theory about why she had extended the invitation.

But now that we were here talking about Dorothy Parker and Virginia Woolf and just about everything but cooking, the whole idea seemed ludicrous. She obviously could care less if we knew anything at all about food, which, judging from our recent skirmishes with croissants and herb vinegars, we didn't. In fact, when the subject of cooking schools came up, she had nothing too complimentary to say. They were "terribly costly," mere "social groups, really," and had nothing to do with cooking so far as she was concerned. All they really need is a staff of hairdressers "for the bedraggled heiresses from Texas who enroll in those classes." So we just stayed around the table awhile longer munching on cookies and sipping our wine and talking about everything, whether it was edible or not.

We felt amazingly comfortable, as if we had known each other from somewhere before. Perhaps it was the literature we shared, much of it Mary Frances's. Though we were half her age, she spoke easily with us, seemingly without hesitation, her voice soothing and gentle, as if she were saying only nice things. Actually the opposite was true. How she spoke bore no resemblance to what she was saying. Her criticism of any ostentation or injustice was merciless; her analyses of people she didn't care for left them not a shred of vestigial goodness. She was probably dead right in most of her soft-spoken invectives. She struck me as the kind of person who was always, as we used to say in Brooklyn, the first kid on the block: whatever you came up with, she already had it or knew about it or had been there.

In my miniature diary, which allows only one inch of recorded activities per day, I did manage to fit in another comment from this October day in 1977: "She appeared to like us; we spoke of the worlds of poems, food; we all liked each other."

The three of us did not get together again before the trip to France. Instead of going directly to Grasse, I stopped at Cannes first, to see what I could of the film festival. Simone Beck had told me to call her from the train station, which was not far from her, and she would pick me up there. I was enchanted with the idea of seeing the Cannes train station, to which Mary Frances had traveled so often from the Gare de Lyon. Her description of the journey in *As They Were* was so full of motion, the train sliding "southward through the forests and farms . . . with cliffs and twisted pines and strange villas, until I got to the familiar little station in Cannes. . . ." Be sure to notice every little thing about the station, I instructed myself, so you can give Mary Frances an update when you get back, since she can't be here herself.

Once at the station, the first thing I noticed was the row of public telephones. It struck me as both surprising and inconsiderate that the instructions for making a call were printed in French, as if this were a deliberate plot to baffle the monolingual tourist. I did finally get the phone to ring, somewhere, but the voice that answered was not Simone Beck's. To my astonishment, however, I had reached the correct number, and the woman did have a message for me from Simca, albeit in French. Until then I hadn't realized that my facility with French depended more on pantomime than on anything that could be communicated over a phone. Eventually I got the point that Simca would be delayed; she would not be able to pick me up until after 6:00 P.M. But I should wait for her at the station until she got there. Today she was having lunch in Aix-en-Provence with M. F. K. Fisher.

I was surprised at first. I had no idea she would be here. But then, how would I know; why should she tell me? It had nothing to do with me, except that now I would have to hang around a little longer at the railroad station in Cannes. I pulled off my backpack and snuggled next to it on one of the long benches. I wondered what she was having for lunch over there in Aix; considering the circumstances, I felt I had a right to know. When we get back to California, we'll talk about that, I thought, among other things.

Navettes
for Mrs. Fisher

"Bring something silly," she suggested. "Or bring dessert."

That seemed easy enough. She would take care of the lunch and the wine. Maybe she would even warm up a handful of almonds, the way she sometimes did, and then bundle them in the folds of her French tea towel set in an olive-wood bowl. "Something silly": it was one of those suggestions that couldn't have been more informal, or more intimidating.

If only she herself weren't so impeccable about these things; if only she weren't someone who cared as much about what you put in your mouth as whom you were with at the time and whether it was raining. Silly, but not like jelly beans or glazed doughnuts. Silly, not ridiculous.

Cookies seemed appropriately informal. But which of the world's millions of recipes was the right one to make for her? From her writings, especially *The Gastronomical Me, Serve It Forth,* and *A Considerable Town,* I knew that she had spent a good part of her life in the south of France. In several roles—as a young woman just married; as a seasoned, life-savoring writer, and as a mother of two young girls—she had lived there, in Dijon, in Aix-en-Provence, in Marseille, and had mixed the stories of those places with her own. She might enjoy some honest French cookies, not the showy ones that look like pearl-studded broaches or the latches on satin evening bags: they weren't her style. She'd say they were too beautiful to eat, and then she would tell about other things she has known that were too beautiful to eat, and then she wouldn't eat them.

Whatever I chose, it had to be absolutely correct: intellectually, culturally, personally. I was seeking a cookie with so many levels of meaning that she would know at a glance the great measure of thought behind it. I wanted to please her, not with my baking abilities, which were unremarkable, but with my informed appreciation. I was looking for the recipe that would show her my sensitivity to her life, my gratitude for what she had so generously shared of it in her writings. And I wanted it to taste good, or I'd never hear the end of it.

I began by researching the subject, raiding the cookie jargon for its *drops, crescents,* and *twists,* uncovering the ethnic identities of uncanny batters and ingredients. Many cookies seemed nice enough, but none was truly relevant. The only recipe even remotely apropos bore the unfortunate name Gallic goodies. I knew she was not the Gallic goodies type. My sense of perspective was disappearing even faster than my sense of humor when I happened to come across, hidden in the back of Richard Olney's *Simple French Food,* an entire section devoted to the little Christmas cakes of Provence.

Even better, the Provençal conception of Christmas seemed to last forever, at least as far as cookies were concerned. There were specific confections designed to commemorate miracles and assorted mystical activities right on through to Candlemas Day, the second of February. On that day a simple buttery cookie called *navette de la Chandeleur* was baked all over Marseille: a most considerable cookie, I thought, knowing better than to say it aloud, then or ever. Surely she would know of these *navettes*. She had traveled so often to Marseille, and food was always so central to her special perspective on the life of everything. Whatever Candlemas Day was, it was just about that time of year now. And whether or not anybody in Marseille was still making *navettes* for the occasion, I was certainly going to do so in California.

Since the word *navette* appeared to be a form of *navet*, the word for turnip, for a while I tried to figure out whether the cookie was supposed to be shaped like a turnip. Perhaps *navettes* symbolized the winter harvest, a belated homage to root vegetables. The word *Chandeleur* was equally intriguing. Ah, Marseille and its mysteries, I thought, where the rough coexists with the regal, the turnip with the chandelier. Most important, I knew I was doing the right thing. This was no mere batch of cookies: this was transcendence, palpable communication between me and the past, her past. I couldn't wait for her to open the tin into which I had carefully packed my *navettes*, or our *navettes* as I had begun to think of them, allowing myself a bit of nostalgia by proxy. The recipe made twelve; I made twenty-four. The next day, when I tucked the little tin next to me for the drive north to Sonoma, it still felt warm.

The woman who was leaving as I pulled in the driveway had no doubt just delivered a batch of her very own homegrown onion compote. She had that kind of smile on her face. People were forever bringing Mary Frances things like red-pepper marmalades or a day's gathering of fleshy, brash chanterelles. The kitchen drainboard, the heavy refectory table, and even the couch were always laden with harvests of things that had probably just been dropped off unexpectedly, since they seldom got incorporated into that day's lunch. A quick glance proved that today was no exception, though a lot of something was going into the oven as I walked in.

She didn't hear me. I tried to cough in a nonstartling way, but she was taking something off the top of the stove. It looked like a wrought-iron tree with holes in the branches, each of which held a blue-white egg. As she set it down on top of a pile of mail, I decided it was time for a big cough.

"Is that you, dear?" she said, turning around. "I thought it was Charlie shuffling around over there. He's always packing himself into some cozy corner, purring and fussing."

Her cheeks were the color that is meant when anyone speaks of healthy pink cheeks.

"I'm so happy to see you; you look beautiful. It's been too long again."

She was either finished with what she was doing, or she was finished with it for the duration. It was one of her gifts to turn herself fully to the moment, to cleave herself from what she had been doing before. Once she gave you her attention, you had it, all of it, the undivided kind, for better or for worse.

We had our wine and, from the wood-burning stove, the delicious warm fire that was, on this rain-chilled Tuesday noon, the only thing better than almonds. It was one of those days so nasty that everyone unites against it. No one holds out and tries to make a case for how refreshing it is to have a day like this once in a while. With the weather as our scapegoat, a mood of agreeability set in, and we soon found ourselves assenting on matters which, on a nicer day, would surely have started some good arguments. It was into this atmosphere of universal acceptance that I introduced my turnips.

"When you were in Marseille around this time of year," so coyly I began, "did you ever hear of a local confection called *navettes de la Chandeleur?*"

"*Navettes!*" she echoed, before I'd finished mispronouncing the last syllable. I could almost hear her mind loading up the appropriate reel of *navette*-entangled memories. Her gray eyes sparkled, sharpening the focus, getting the details as clear and current as the present moment. She was a veritable genius at this kind of recall. "*Navettes!* Oh, yes! They were awful!"

Awful?

"They were little cookies. They were made only in two places in Marseille, and at one time I lived directly above one of them."

Awful?

"They were hard as bricks. Inedible, really. People would buy them every year for Candlemas Day, and the next year they would still have them from the year before. They were so hard and dry they kept all year. The Candlemas ceremony itself was quite lovely, though, flickering with white and green candles. That Provence green: you only see it there."

With any luck the things she associated with *navettes* would be pleasant. That could brighten her interpretation considerably. I had noticed that what she remembered depended less on the events themselves than on how she was feeling when she remembered them. I ventured to move what I thought was forward.

"Well, what about the turnips? Why were the cookies named after turnips?"

"Turnips!" she echoed, her brow, even her voice, furrowed. The cat that never left the room ran out into the rain.

"I thought perhaps that the word *navettes* was a variation of *navets*. I mean, maybe the shape or something. Olney doesn't elaborate," I added weakly. Blame it on him.

"*Navettes* refer to the little boat in which Mary Magdalene was supposed to have come to Marseille. That's why the cookies are shaped that way. Like little canoes with hooks on either end. The slit down the center is the inside of the boat."

How does she know all this? I wondered. Maybe she's wrong. So what if she *is* wrong? What good would that do? Was I going to tell her? I could go look it up and write back and tell her she was wrong. Then what? She seemed to have made it her business to know the most amazing minutiae: the difference between corn pone and johnnycakes, what grits really are (or is), how truffles grow. And then she gives you the works: the mythology, the politics, the gastronomy, and any other relevant details, all rolled into one.

Right now she was profoundly into *navettes,* unfortunately. Too profoundly for my good.

My mind chased away images of the bifurcated turnips waiting in the tin. I think it was the way I said, "Oh," that made her ask, "Why all this curiosity about *navettes* anyway?"

"Oh, well, it was just that I came across this recipe, and I thought maybe since it was about that time of the year and Marseille and everything. And since you did mention about bringing something silly . . ." Silly, I remembered, not preposterous.

"You mean you made *navettes?* You actually made them? I can't imagine anyone making those bone-dry, impenetrable stones. I suppose they could be made edible, though it wouldn't be consistent with the way they actually were."

I had never thought of food that way before: some

things by nature or tradition are not terribly delicious, and it is not our place, we who are interested in food, to "improve" them, to alter the attributes that give them their own special faults. I knew there was nothing wrong with the cookies in the tin; that was the problem. When she found out that they were in fact delicious, she would have to be disappointed. She would realize that the recipe had been bastardized, that it had sacrificed truth for taste. The idea is not to make something taste good if it doesn't but, rather, to make something else altogether. That's the trouble with cookbooks and photographs and art in general: despite all the best intentions, the artist gets in the way.

I felt better after this split-second philosophizing. I was an innocent bystander after all. I could dump it all on Olney for caring more about pleasure than history. Anyway, I could see by her pursed lips that she was planning to enter into this *navettes* reverie, no matter how unfaithful this particular reproduction. She was squinting meaningfully into the tin.

"*Navettes*," she said, looking them over like a litter of unpedigreed kittens. "All over Marseille on the days around Candlemas you could smell them cooking. It was the orange peel, the bitter Seville orange peel they folded into the dough. That was the characteristic thing about *navettes.*"

Damn Olney. He obviously lived over the *other* place that made *navettes* in Marseille. Those bakers either didn't like Mary Magdalene (some people don't) or didn't care a hoot about whether she had oranges in her boat. I proceeded cautiously.

"What if," I ventured, "there were no orange peel in the recipe? What would you say of that?"

"No orange peel?" She was bewildered.

"I mean, wouldn't you say that was silly?"

"No," she said. "Not necessarily."

EPILOGUE

Incredible though it may seem, after allowing a decent interval to pass, I ventured another batch of *navettes*. The day after I brought them to Mary Frances, I received the following note:

> January 18, 1983
>
> I worked my way through another navette after you . . . left! I really find them good, in a tough but subtle way, . . . sortakinda like the people of Marseille! Norah's coming tomorrow, and I'll surprise her with them. (You left a lot. . . . Tomorrow I'll also give a couple to my little godson Andrew, going on three. I think they are rather naive, like children.)
>
> I looked at the recipe in my trusty *Cuisinière Provençale*, by Reboul. (Do you have a copy of that? It's a jewel, . . . still published every year in Marseille, in facsimile. . . .)

The ingredients are flour, powdered sugar,
butter, pinch of salt, grated zest of lemon, eggs and
water.
    I think Norah will agree with me that the
ones we walked past several times a day in
Marseille had orange instead of lemon in them. . . .
They smelled very sweet . . . much better than they
were.

Too late I rediscovered what I had once read and somehow forgotten: Mary Frances's own words on the subject of *navettes,* which appear all too conspicuously in *A Considerable Town:* "I ate a lot of navettes, little boat-shaped cookies, tough dough tasting vaguely of orange peel, smelling better than they are. They are supposed to symbolize the miraculous vessel Magdalene and all other saints piloted to safety near Marseille. I did not much like the little pastries."

Adventures in Eating:

Room Service

"**C**an you and Peter join me for dinner at the Stanford Court?" It was Mary Frances on the phone, explaining that she would be coming down from Glen Ellen to stay in San Francisco for several days. She always stayed at the Stanford Court Hotel, which reminded me, for no demonstrable reason, of the Plaza. It was much more West Coast, its halls less hallowed perhaps, its manner less ossified. But it was the kind of place that no longer pleaded innocence. I suspected it may even have its own California Eloise, the little girl who lived at the Plaza Hotel and survived mainly on two magic words: *room service*. Eloise could think of anything in the world—even chocolate ice cream with strawberries and cherries and chocolate sauce and honey and jelly beans and two cookies and one raisin stuck into it—and room service would bring it right up.

I doubted Mary Frances was inviting us for an evening of room service, although you could never be certain with her. Probably we would eat in the hotel restaurant, which had a cavernous stone oven that you could see from certain special tables. The way they roasted lamb there made it taste as if it were turned over open fires and smoky rosemary branches on a Greek mountainside.

"Yes," I said, feeling instantly festive. "Certainly, yes."

She said she would be inviting some other people also but wanted us to come to her room first "for drinks and nibbles."

I loved going to the Stanford Court when she was there. The last time she invited us to the hotel, she hosted a lively dinner party in one of the small private dining rooms. Besides us she had assembled some of her wide array of friends: a few people from a California publishing company; a woman who worked in a Berkeley bookstore; someone who was either starting up or closing down a cooking school—I can't remember the exact stage since he accomplished both feats in a relatively short time; a woman who arranged talks for the San Francisco library and her husband, who was something corporate and was often on business trips or in meetings but was "fortunately able to make it this evening," as he put it. But most imposing of all, there was Norah, Mary Frances's sister. She looked like she thought this was quite a big fuss to be making over a meal, but maybe it was because she was sitting at the far end of the table and I couldn't hear exactly what she was saying. We didn't get any menus for the longest time. Someone thought they were looking for a waiter skinny enough to fit between the chairs and the wall. Finally instead of menus we got potatoes and caviar and champagne, followed by *poussin* with crushed coriander and then big slices of chocolate cake. Mary Frances had taken care of planning the meal, so we could just continue eating and talking about books or cooking or libraries, while trying to hear Norah at the other end of the table.

Mary Frances seemed to be completely in charge of the entire place. It was like her very own private hotel, especially the suite of rooms on the eighth floor she always stayed in. She called this gloriously grand hotel "the old watering hole" in order to de-emphasize its luxuriousness, but it was hard to miss.

This time Peter and I were determined to get there in plenty of time for our "drinks and nibbles" so we could have a few minutes with her before everyone else arrived. We walked into the glittering lobby, with its jewelry-display cases and guests in magazine-ad clothes—even the most informally dressed children were outfitted head to toe in Esprit logos. It was late afternoon. People were gathering in the lobby, gazing with prurient interest at the beautiful tiny sculpted cakes on a cart—as elegant as the lobby jewels—but ordering instead a martini or champagne. I glanced over because there was always "someone" there, usually an author or two on the West Coast leg of a tour for their newest book being interviewed by some TV news reporter or someone from *The Bay Guardian* or possibly even the *San Francisco Chronicle*. It might be John Irving, Elizabeth Taylor, Leon Uris, or Roger Vergé. And they would always be saying that this was the best part of their tour, being in San Francisco; they wished they could stay a few extra days so they could go to "that great little hidden

away [of course] restaurant" they remembered not from
last time they were here, but from the first time. Usually
the place had either closed down or changed completely or
been turned into an International House of Pancakes. I
once interviewed Calvin Trillin in the Stanford Court
shortly after the publication of *Alice, Let's Eat.* The interview never resulted in an article, but I did learn something:
it's hard to write about writers who write about themselves, because they've already set down everything they
want you to know. This was also the case with Mary
Frances.

Squinting into the darkness, I did see someone I knew.
She was wrapped in bright swirls of blue and green, like
sapphires and emeralds, set against the platinum of her
hair. It was Mary Frances. She would have looked like a
queen surveying her gardens except for one thing. Her
perfectly composed porcelain-doll face changed instantly
when she saw us, to a look that can only be called goofy.
She raised her eyebrows, fluttered her lids, and sucked in
her cheeks. We did likewise; we had that effect on each
other. It was as though we were trespassers trying to play
our parts in our fancy duds but unable to keep up the
pretense in front of each other. Maybe it was because we
were writers who understand that possibly the sole advantage of our masochistic profession is that you don't have to
get dressed in the morning. ("Install me in any profession / save this damn'd profession of writing," prayed Ezra
Pound once, possibly in his pajamas, "where one needs
one's brains all the time.")

Peter was already folding her into a hug. We all kissed and fussed, surprised, for some reason, to find each other exactly where we were all supposed to be.

"You're early," she said, as if caught off guard.

"The traffic was horrible," Peter explained, "but not horrible enough."

"What are you doing in the lobby, anyway?" I asked. "Loitering?"

The thought of M. F. K. Fisher loitering anywhere got us all giggling, heartily but respectably.

"I'm actually waiting for Mary Jane," she said, mumbling about how the room wasn't ready; it was "never quite ready." As we looked toward the glass doors leading in from the parking lot, Mary Jane appeared on the other side, dragging behind her something that looked like a folded-up wheelchair. She was a short elf of a person, a smidgen over five feet tall, but she had strong arms, a square build, and a general midwestern toughness that showed in the set of her jaw. In the relatively short time she had been working for Mary Frances, helping around the house, doing the driving and accompanying her on excursions of any length, Mary Jane had made it possible for Mary Frances to travel more widely and more often than she had been doing in recent years. Mary Frances had been experiencing some hip and knee problems, which were aggravated by the kind of activities she'd refused to curtail—feeding the cats, for example, or kicking the door shut. Mary Jane took care of these and more strenuous matters as well, such as handling the wheelchair she was now setting up, simultaneously greeting us and shaking hands all around.

"Did Mary Frances tell you where we were?" she asked, only slightly breathless.

"No. Actually we just this minute arrived ourselves," I answered, noticing out of the corner of my eye that Mary Frances had taken Peter's arm and was leading him toward the desk. Their backs were turned to us, and they seemed to be staring directly at a light on the wall.

"Have you ever noticed this?" she was asking.

I went over and peeked in front of them. On the wall was a small oil painting of an old gnarled birch tree, lit by a shaded brass lamp mounted above. When my eyes adjusted, I could make out the name: Maxfield Parrish.

"People are always getting mixed up," she was saying, "thinking it was Maxfield I was married to."

Actually she was married in the late 1930s to Maxfield's cousin Dillwyn Parrish, the great passion of her young life, of all her life, as it turned out. She often insists that his interest in her earliest literary efforts encouraged her to continue writing seriously. Although he himself is the subject, directly or indirectly, of much of her writing, she seldom uses his name. Perhaps this is her writer's way of protecting her privacy, keeping something for herself. She refers to him as Timmy or Chexbres.

"In Switzerland, where we were living," she explained, "*chexbres* means "goat." Timmy looked like a goat from the side, you know. I think goats are very beautiful."

At their Swiss farm, which they called Paquis, meaning "pasture," they wrote stories together, even a light novel, *Touch and Go.* She completed her second book, *Consider the Oyster,* which she was to dedicate to her beloved. By the time it was published in 1941, Dillwyn was dead. His illness, called Buerger's disease, had required the amputation of one leg and left him in constant and excruciating pain. Facing the prospect of further amputation, Dillwyn took his own life. His artistic influence extends to the present-day efforts of Mary Frances's grandson, Chris, who proudly signs his cartoon drawings C. Parrish.

During their brief marriage Dillwyn painted the lyrical portraits of flowers and trees that now fill Mary Frances's walls and "art closet" in Glen Ellen. But what he really wanted to do, according to Mary Frances, was to fight the fascists in Spain.

"Did you know the reason why Timmy worked as a counterspy and general kidnapper of rare drawings from the Prado was that he was considered too old for the Lincoln Battalion? It almost broke his heart. I think getting all those Goyas and Picassos out was a pretty good job, though. . . ."

Her voice went dry for a moment but immediately revived into a bright chirp of words. "He managed to risk his life anyway, working with the underground smuggling art out of the country. He did it with his umbrella." She paused long enough to make us wonder, but not so long that we had to ask. "By rolling the canvases up around the ferrule of his umbrella and smuggling them into neutral Switzerland, where we were living in Vevey." When Geneva held an exhibition of the Prado masterpieces in 1939, she explained, they were able to see some of the works he had rescued.

"When we were in the Basque country a few years after Franco died," Peter began, "we met a man in Bilbao named Patricio de la Sota." She looked up immediately; how could she not be interested in a man named Patricio? Peter described how in the 1930s the Franco regime had taken everything from Patricio's family, including their home, which was turned into the most palatial police station in the Basque country. The day we were there Patricio received a mysterious giant parcel, part of the family property that had been confiscated forty years before. We brought it to an upstairs room and started to pull off the wrapping paper. A period of impatient ripping and tearing quickly ensued and just as quickly ceased when we saw suddenly that it was a painting by El Greco. Patricio's face went pale. He looked over at his old uncle, who was standing with us. Now in his eighties, the uncle had spent half his life combating Franco in one form or another. This was not art but heritage being restored, literally. It was an amazing moment.

Mary Frances was shaking her head, as if she were familiar with that kind of moment. We looked at each other, kindred through time, beyond the confines of the mere half dozen years we had known each other. She was standing there with Timmy and utterly without him.

After another long but unembarrassed minute, Mary Frances sat down in the wheelchair, and we went up in the elevator to the eighth floor. We got to the room, and Mary Jane opened the door. It looked the same as ever: the big living room with grand mirrors and wallpaper and important-looking dark furniture, grandmother's-house furniture—marble-topped end tables, lamps of great stature with prima-donna shades that might have had silky fringes on their edges but didn't. There were other rooms as well, a few bedrooms, maybe even a kitchen way back inside; I wasn't sure. It was like being in a house.

"I was here in this room once when you weren't, you know, Mary Frances," I began, trying to sound provocative.

"Oh?" she said with a question mark, interested.

"I came here to talk to James Beard for a story I wanted to write about his favorite eating places in San Francisco. I remember he was sitting right where you are, on the couch."

I looked over and imagined him there, filling up much more of the couch than Mary Frances did. Four Mary Frances could have fit in that one James Beard space. He had been wearing a red plaid shirt and the biggest, bluest blue jeans I'd ever seen. He was much bigger than I'd imagined, and jollier and friendlier as well.

"He reminded me of a statue of Paul Bunyan I once saw when I lived in Minnesota," I told Mary Frances.

"In New York they called him Beardo," she informed me, "and sometimes Fatso. But just in fun."

He looked like a drawing, I told her, a cartoon. He chuckled a lot and told me a few funny stories. The best one was about the time he was staying in this corner suite, and Julia Child had the corner suite just above and Craig Claiborne, the one just below.

" 'I remember thinking,' " he recalled, with a husky guffaw, 'that if something happened to this corner of the Stanford Court Hotel that weekend, a big chunk of the American food establishment would be gone in one fell swoop.' Then he laughed and coughed a little and offered me some fruit."

I looked at the bowl of fruit on the table in front of Mary Frances. "In fact it looked like exactly the same bowl of fruit, except maybe they had no kiwis then. At least I don't remember making fun of kiwis, and I'm sure we would have, considering how well we got along. It must have been eight or nine years ago."

"Yes, well, he wasn't in very good shape that time. And they made him do too many things." With that Mary Frances tipped the bowl of fruit toward me while Mary Jane remarked on the fruit's perfect ripeness.

"They give you so much beautiful fruit. Usually we put it in one of the shower caps and take it home," Mary Jane confessed with a peek at Mary Frances to see if she should have told about that.

"Sure. Why not?" I said, as Mary Frances handed me a bunch of the tiniest grapes I'd ever seen. They looked like a child's necklace.

"Currants," she said.

"I don't remember these either," I smiled, gobbling them down, "but I do recall his long disquisition on the first time he was in San Francisco, for the Pacific Panama Exposition, in 1915. He came down with his family from Oregon, I believe."

Mary Frances said, "something like that," and that her early memories of San Francisco also centered on the Pacific Panama Exposition, even though it wasn't she who came. She was only nine years old. It was her parents, who traveled up from Whittier to visit San Francisco, discover its restaurants, and attend the exposition. The souvenirs and mementos they brought back conveyed a sense of magic about San Francisco, an aura that the city retained for their little daughter. Going up to San Francisco from Whittier or Palo Alto when she was a young girl or traveling down to San Francisco from Saint Helena when she was the mother of her own young girls, even for an appointment with the orthodontist, a trip to the city was always what she called an event. In fact, the only time San Francisco lost its attraction for her was when she actually lived in it.

"We had come back from Provence, my girls and me. Anne was thirteen; Kennedy, ten. We also had a French girl, Monique, with us. We were all living in an apartment smack next to that Christian Science church with the famous organ that played that awful Christian Science music that made the walls of our apartment tremble." She paused to shudder, visibly, at the aftershock. "The girls were going to a public school that wouldn't allow them to cross Van Ness Avenue or play in the playground nearby. I suppose they thought there'd be satyrs under the trees. Well, there were satyrs under the trees in Provence, too. Who cares?"

Mary Jane nodded, commenting that San Francisco seemed to be changing a lot lately. She and Mary Frances had just returned from a sad meeting with a young man, newly arrived in San Francisco, who had AIDS. He had been writing to Mary Frances for some time and wanted to meet her. Mary Jane and Mary Frances drove to Fisherman's Wharf and had coffee with him. He told them he was in despair, that he knew no one in the area. Mary Frances gave him some names of people who could help and told him about the organizations in the city that assisted people with AIDS. Not only did she know quite a bit about these organizations and groups, she supported them with more than verbal encouragement. In fact, some time later, when she was awarded the Fred Cody Memorial Award, a literary prize presented by the San Francisco Bay Area Book Reviewers Association, she instructed that the five-hundred-dollar prize money be sent directly to a benefit for people with AIDS.

Someone was knocking at the door.

Mary Jane opened it and greeted the visitor with hugs and handshakes. But he seemed to be leaving before he had walked completely into the room. He just wanted to make sure all was well, he was trying to say.

"This is Jim Nassikas," Mary Frances called to us as we shook our heads in recognition; we had met several times. I don't know how he remembered half the people he was introduced to. He was president of the Stanford Court Hotel and a great friend of Mary Frances, and he was always urging her to come to the city and stay at the Stanford Court. It was he who had purchased the Parrish painting for the lobby.

"It's called *The Old Birch,*" he said, explaining that its enchantment for him was its similarity to all the old birches in New Hampshire near his hometown. After he left the comfortable, rusty-gold autumns of New England, he told us, he attended the same hotel and restaurant school in Switzerland as Mary Frances's friend Craig Claiborne.

"That's where I first met Craig," he said nostalgically. These friendships went back whole lifetimes, I thought; Peter and I are definitely the new kids on this particular block. I wanted to ask him to send someone to forcibly remove my hand from the Hawaiian potato chips because they were too delicious: I couldn't stop eating them.

The doorbell was ringing again. It was Frances Steele, another long-time friend of Mary Frances, who was joining us for dinner. I thanked her for sending me *Delmonico's,* a book about the famous New York restaurant and the family that founded it. It was written by her late husband, Bob Steele, using the name Lately Thomas. I had seen many of his other books, whose subjects ranged from Thomas Jefferson to Senator Joseph McCarthy, on Mary Frances's bookshelves.

Behind Frances Steele two more people materialized: Pat and Marsha Moran, who lived near Mary Frances and worked with her at least once a week taking dictation and typing her notes and correspondence.

Before long we had all eaten too many potato chips.

"Shall we eat?" Mary Frances asked, as if we hadn't been doing that all along.

Mary Jane made a phone call, and someone magically appeared at the door to take Mary Frances and her unruly little dinner party down to Fourneau Ovens via a special service elevator near her room that was large enough for both the wheelchair and the guest list. I now knew why Mary Frances, attempting to deluxuriate her digs, referred to her suite as "the dingy pad by the elevator shaft." When we emerged from the elevator and scampered through the kitchens and pantries and storage rooms, I got the feeling of being backstage. After a series of surprisingly unexciting hotel secrets, I discovered a wall of what looked like cages. I almost expected them to contain pet gerbils or sleeping turtles or at least toy poodles. But they held, instead, wine. Each compartment was labeled with a name—the name of the wine's owner, I was informed—who was assured by such a system that the prized wine would always be on the premises when he (or, less likely, she) was.

Nobody seemed to be releasing any pet wines from their cages as we tiptoed—for some reason no one could explain—past the cages. Soon we were led to a table at the side of the restaurant with curved, bubbly windows that made us feel as if we were walking into a greenhouse. There was a lot of confusion as we sidled in, pulled out chairs, and tried to sit next to whomever Mary Frances wanted us to sit next to. Soon everything was restored to the previous level of chaos, except for two problems: there were no potato chips, and we could hardly hear each other.

The acoustics in this tunnellike location were exception-
ally effective in gathering in the noise and chatter from
nearby tables while filtering out the most stentorian attempts at our own table. After several minutes of reading
lips, Mary Frances called a waiter over. He had to bend
almost in half to hear her words. When he finally did hear
them, he looked mortified, as did the bevy of other restaurant personnel who came over to rectify this situation, a
complaint from M. F. K. Fisher. You could see by their
concern they knew they were going to be reviewing this
unfortunate turn of events with the management the following morning.

The next thing we were all doing was getting up,
shuffling around, bumping along behind each other, back
into the hotel's private parts again—were they going to
feed us in the kitchen?—past the dessert racks and dish-
washing machines. Did they have a secret room among
these nether regions? Or was Mary Frances going to cart
us off to another restaurant?

But we didn't seem to be going anywhere except back
into the big freight elevator that had delivered us. We all
contributed to the general complaints about the noise.
Mary Frances proposed, since there were no free tables,
that we go back to her room and have our dinner there. She
sounded apologetic about it, as if we would be disappointed. No apologies could have been heard anyway above
the din of excitement that her suggestion created; this was
getting to be an adventure. And an adventure, almost any
adventure, was better than a mere perfect meal. I was sure

Mary Frances would agree with that in principle, although her concerned expression suggested that she might not be so enthusiastic about the idea at the moment, what with all these hungry dinner guests on her hands. For myself, I was almost unruly with anticipation that this might mean those longed-for magic words: *room service.*

Back in her suite, my hopes were further sparked by seeing Mary Frances pick up the room-service menu tucked under one of the lamps.

"Mary Frances, does this mean," I ventured tentatively, afraid if I outguessed her, she would surely change her mind, "that we get to order our meal from the room-service menu?"

Mary Frances looked up, her eyes sharpening, on the alert.

"I hope not," she said, tossing the menu aside. "It doesn't look too interesting. Look for yourself, dear."

I felt like saying it didn't make any difference, that the important thing was to call room service and order anything so we could watch them wheel it in on lovely silver trays and say, *"Bonjour, Eloise. Voici votre petit déjeuner,"* or words to that effect. But she felt this sense of responsibility, I could see that, and I did have to admit that the room-service menu was not as exciting as the real restaurant menu: no "catch of the day" or sauté of three kinds of fresh wild mushrooms.

"I see what you mean," I said weakly.

"Do you think you could call down and ask them if we

could order from the restaurant menu? Then everyone could have what they wanted anyway."

"Of course," I answered, possibly too eager. What an idea! Who would ever have thought of anything so fortuitous? A whole full-blown, ultraprofessional restaurant squeezed into room service. As I picked up the phone, I felt the burden of responsibility climb silently onto my shoulders. If I could get them to say yes, it would be even better than room service at the Plaza.

"Hello, this is M. F. K. Fisher's room," I began, choosing my words carefully. I could feel those fox-fur gray eyes listening. "Our party, the Fisher party, was just down there in the restaurant for dinner, and *we couldn't hear ourselves think*"—might as well rub it in—"so we came back to *M. F. K. Fisher's suite* and decided to order from the room-service menu, but . . . ,"—and now I decided to change into my *How to Win Friends and Influence People* portion of the program—"it was so, well, different from your wonderful Fourneau Ovens menu, and since we all had our hearts set on something already . . ."

Before I could finish, the gentleman on the line was saying of course, whatever we wanted; they'd be only happy to. They would bring up some Fourneau Ovens menus so we could decide.

I smiled at Mary Frances so she would know all was well. She took my hand and patted it, obviously satisfied. A wave of relief rippled through the room as people realized that the end of delayed gratification was in sight. This was the most sensitive, certainly the most gracious hotel in San Francisco, we all agreed. Mary Frances gave all the credit to Jim Nassikas.

"People love the man," she told me as my fingers worked their way back into their accustomed position among the potato chips, "especially the people who work for him." The hotel was owned and run by people, that was the thing, she emphasized, not some impersonal, mammoth corporation.

"Even the rugs," she said, looking suddenly guilty, as if a confession were forthcoming. It was only a dream, though, she admitted before she began, but the previous night she'd had this wonderful fantasy of careening up and down the hallways in the wheelchair at breakneck speed, past the cleaning people's towel wagons, around corners, everywhere. She'd tried it out "a little, just here in the room," she revealed, but it didn't work at all. "The rugs are too thick," she said with a chuckling smile.

Ironically this genteel establishment was bought soon afterward by one of those very corporations, an event followed by the departure of Mr. Nassikas and some loyal employees. One of them, the pastry chef Jim Dodge, would remember Mary Frances's visits to the hotel fondly, mentioning how they had a sort of tradition to make sure that her room was never ready.

"What do you mean 'never ready'?" I asked.

"One time she happened to arrive before her room was ready," he explained. "We suggested that she have a cocktail in the lounge while she waited. She seemed to have such a nice time doing that. So from then on when she arrived, we would tell her her room wasn't ready, and she would go have a martini." She didn't drink standard martinis as far as I knew; she drank only her favorite blend of wine and something else mixed to a color—just short of fuchsia—that is usually associated with cough medicine. It may even have tasted like cough medicine, considering the way she took it down, in tiny, unconvincing sips.

As I stared at the overly thick rug, Mary Jane appeared, handing one of those freshly made pink-colored drinks to Mary Frances. The rest of us were doing away with the white wine, a small plate of olives, the currants, and whatever else in the fruit basket might be considered a first course. We had ordered our meals and were waiting for their delivery when Peter and I suddenly realized that we would have to be leaving very soon. We had promised our baby-sitter "no later than 10:30." I told Mary Frances that we must be out the door in twenty minutes no matter what. She looked concerned but not too concerned: she knew this was already a great dinner party even without the food.

Then there was a knock on the door. Three men in stiff-looking white suits pushed in some wheeled contraptions made of industrial aluminum, with handles and hinges and appendages that they immediately pulled out or up or down or under. The men looked like hospital attendants at first. They began converting their tanklike vehicles into dinner tables covered with linen and held down by heavy-handled silver forks and knives and crystal salt and pepper shakers. Now they seemed more like magicians as they snapped their fingers to conjure up the requisite number of chairs and whisked off the silver domed tops of platters laden with sautéed wild mushrooms piled on lettuce leaves. We ate the first courses in nineteen and a half minutes and then, duck in ginger chile sauce or no duck in ginger chile sauce, we had to leave. With equal regret we said good-bye to our fellow guests and to the crisp-skinned duck. But Mary Frances had other ideas: take it with you, she urged, and sheets of aluminum foil materialized.

By the time the elevator reached the main floor, we realized we were really late. We started to run through the lobby, two disheveled characters with coattails flapping, armed with suspicious-looking bulging aluminum bundles, huffing and puffing and smelling like ginger chile sauce.

We made it home almost exactly on time, paid the baby-sitter, and collapsed into the big, puffy pillows on the floor in front of the fireplace.

"Another madcap Mary Frances day," I said, once I caught my breath. We pulled the coffee table over and unwrapped our respective ducks. Their warming spiciness gushed into the room. I pulled off a strip of crinkly skin.

"Would you like a knife and fork?" Peter asked with a knowing grin.

"Maybe later," I answered.

When we finished, all that was left of our dinner were two pieces of aluminum.

"This is really the ultimate room service, don't you

think?" I asked, licking my fingers. "I think we got the best of it."

"Yes," Peter replied. "Mary Frances probably thinks so too."

Noni
and Doty

She knew a lot of psychiatry and she was tall. That was about all we knew about Norah. But it was the chance of seeing the two of them together that got us driving all over blazes. That and the fact that we didn't realize just how far Jenner was.

"I'll be at my sister Norah's in Jenner the day you and Peter were planning to visit," Mary Frances told us, her voice over the phone sounding distressed. "But Norah would love you to come to her place, too, and have lunch with both of us."

We remembered another thing about Norah: what we weren't supposed to call her.

"Noni. I call her Noni. But nobody else calls her Noni." A word to the wise . . .

And Norah called Mary Frances Doty, a nickname for "daughter" that she has sported since birth, possibly in honor of her position as the first-born of the four Kennedy children.

"Is anyone else allowed to call you Doty?" Peter had asked.

"Only children," she had answered quite firmly.

So we knew what we wouldn't call Norah, if we ever found our way through the tangle of tiny roads leading toward the Pacific Ocean. Actually we did find the Pacific Ocean—it's hard to miss—and remembered to keep it on our left. On our right the mountain was a pastiche of rugged rectangular stones capped with moss, like Stone Age castles. Soon we were in Jenner-by-the-Sea (they say it as if it were one word) looking for the volunteer fire department and other landmarks that were supposed to help us find Norah's house. But whoever made up the addresses for the town of Jenner must have been trying to protect everyone's privacy. Either the streets had no names, or the houses had no numbers, or both.

The same defender of privacy must have worked for the phone company, because when we finally found a telephone booth, there was nothing inside. Nothing, not even one of those back-curdling half seats they sometimes put in to discourage long chats on pay phones. The phone company would have a fit if they knew about this, we giggled, the only bright spot in our discouraging search for Willig Road. Since we now couldn't call Norah for directions, we decided to ask at the gas station across the way. The crotchety attendant looked at us as if he were about to mutter "city slickers," and spit out a wad of chewing tobacco. But he only pointed a crooked finger past our noses and said, "Halfway up the hill, right there in front of you."

And there it was, the street, the number, the brown-shingled house, and Norah opening the door. Standing more than six feet tall, she was wearing a white, embroidered sweater over a purple turtleneck and gray slacks. Although she is almost nine years younger than Mary Frances, she seems protective of her big sister, and more serious. Beside her, and a full head shorter, stood Mary Frances, looking playful in her yellow sweatshirt announcing the PHILADELPHIA STRING QUARTET OLYMPIC MUSIC FESTIVAL CONCERTS IN THE BARN, in pink letters. They were both wearing their pewter-gray hair pulled back tightly, parted on the left. Even so, they look so different. It may be their smiles: Norah smiles gently, with a calm sense of propriety. Her eyes are round and steady and keep their distance. Mary Frances gets all her teeth into the process, with a big, jolly curve that dimples her cheeks all the way up to her eyebrows.

We handed over the box of chocolate truffles we had bought from a local candy company that claimed to have invented them. Although we were prepared to repeat the spurious-sounding invention story, we were relieved that Norah took the box from us, no questions asked. Instead we told them about the interesting phone booth. Once inside, I began to understand why Mary Frances often came to Norah's house for refuge, as a hideaway in which she could "get some decent work done on my own book," as she put it.

"I am off to Jenner for a week or so," she had written in a note to me, "and when I come back I will be a new person, firmly detached from the rigors of fan mail, business, etc., etc., . . . or so the script reads now. We'll see!" I knew that Mary Frances received many letters from people who were discovering or rediscovering her books, many of which were being reissued. Although she had always had, as they say, a following, lately there seemed to be a Fisher renaissance afoot. Perhaps it was part of the rediscovery of women artists and writers in general; perhaps it was the food people and young chefs, especially women chefs, who found in her a precedent for what they were trying to do. Or maybe it was because people likcd what she wasn't: she wasn't a chef, she wasn't self-promotional, she wasn't fooled or flattered or tricked by any of it. She was just trying to get some work done. But lately she had been spending four hours a day four days a week answering phone calls and fan mail, all of which was preventing her from doing any serious writing.

"It's strange," she mused, "that this so-called fame which I never sought and don't want takes up so much of my time."

Norah's escape hatch seemed perfect: white walls, wood floor, wood-burning stove; uncluttered, a kind of New England austerity about the place. But if you looked to the right, a wall of windows tempted your eyes to travel down the shrub-covered hill and on to the blue sea, placid except for a passing boat and its trail of watery ruffles and flounces.

In front of one window was a long dining-room table, like a refectory table, on which Norah had set white plates, napkins the color of amethysts, and a vase of flowers that looked like branches draped with short, red fringe. She asked about drinks. We all had the sauvignon blanc that seemed to be waiting for us anyway, except for Mary Frances, who mixed her wine with some cranberry-colored liqueur.

"Is that a kind of *kir?*" Peter asked.

"No; oh, no. Don't like *kir,*" she answered, leading to a full account of Jean Canon Kir, a former mayor of Dijon who was condemned to death because, "when he learned the Germans were coming, he had the town evacuated and the pregnant women housed in the cellars of a winery. When I was living in France, *kir* was cheap, almost the cheapest thing you could drink, *vin blanc* and *cassis.*" She paused to sigh.

"Noni used to drink it," she said, as if she were trying to think of something good to say about it. "But then she was only thirteen at the time."

"Thirteen?"

"Yes. Mother sent Noni to live with us, with Al Fisher and me, in Dijon and Strasbourg. We were so poor then, living in one room. Mother didn't realize how poor we were. So I found a convent where Noni could board and go to school. It was a hard time for everybody. Noni grew up a lot during that time."

For one second, maybe less, their eyes darted across at each other, a reminder of the many years and worlds they had traveled together.

They look a bit like the two mischievous children one imagines they were years ago growing up in Whittier. And yet Mary Frances was almost nine when Norah was born. She called her Baby Norah and said that she snored "like a healthy mouse." It was her other sister, Anne, two years her junior, with whom she went to dancing class, spoke a secret cleft-palate language, and acted out the characters Esmeralda and Jellyanjam. It was Anne who helped devise a way to hold the Sunday-school Bible in front of them so their grandmother would think they were piously following the Scriptures when they were actually reading the funnies. Their only brother, David, was born two years after Norah and became her playmate. They had almost two separate families: the older girls, Mary Frances and Anne, and the decade-younger Norah and David.

Mary Frances was the quintessential big sister, always reading the kids stories and taking them on little excursions and trips. Norah describes her as "a very wonderful older sister. Even though she was away at boarding school a lot, whenever she came home, it was like a celebration."

Only much later, when Norah and Mary Frances were both divorced young women with children, did they really become close friends and traveling companions.

"Of course, everyone was drinking *kirs* on the barge to Burgundy," Mary Frances continued. "Norah and I went on a barge on the Burgundian waterways, about twenty years ago, before it became stylish to take barges."

"Did you know I wrote a poem about barges?" Peter asked, with a dead-giveaway smirk that Mary Frances read instantly as nonserious. "It's not very long. Would you like me . . ."

"Please," replied Mary Frances with a matching smirk.

"Jupiter is very large. / You cannot fit it on a barge."

"Would that be *on* a barge or *in* a barge?" Mary Frances asked, and then continued her story. She and Norah were on a barge, or possibly in a barge, on their way to Les Bastides, Dijon, and Aix, she said. Some people on board recognized Mary Frances and came over to meet her. She turned to introduce Norah. "This is my sister, Mrs. Barr," she said. "Afterward Noni told me she didn't like being my sister. She didn't like being introduced that way."

Norah's face showed no reaction, as if to say that she had forgotten all about all this years ago, but if Mary Frances wanted to continue worrying about it, Norah knew there was nothing she could do. I took the opportunity to ask something that had always intrigued me: how were they able to afford traveling around all those years, especially with five children in tow? Norah, as always, got right to the point: "We had inherited all that lovely money from my father," she said simply.

Judging from the frequency of their travels together, they must have resolved the problem of introductions satisfactorily. Their closeness may have been strengthened because of the death of their siblings. David, an artist and conscientious objector, despondent over the war, committed suicide in 1942 two months after his twenty-third birthday. Their sister, Anne, died of cancer in 1965. Now Norah is, even when she's not around, Mary Frances's constant companion, her one-person reference group.

"And Noni thinks so, too," Mary Frances often says,

referring to just about anything. Norah is the second opinion, often the final opinion.

"Noni says I always burn the toast" was Mary Frances's explanation for why she turned her back on us and set her chair in front of the stove, her eyes intent on its little smoky window.

Norah probably doesn't burn the toast, ever, I thought, looking at her working so efficiently in her spotless, well-ordered kitchen. I was curious about the lunch, the style of it, how it would differ from her sister's. At Mary Frances's things are never this unjumbled. She is always, when one arrives, pulling the leaves off the watercress, cutting the baguettes into croutons, answering the phone, feeding the cat, making a fire, pouring everyone some wine, recounting some tale about a concert she once went to in Dijon or the opening of a winery last Sunday in Napa, usually by somebody "who doesn't know a damn thing about wine."

By contrast, Norah concentrated on the moment and the place: she told us about the birch trees in the yard, the ramshackle structure down the hill that looked as if it were about to tumble into the water, the six-pointed glass star hanging on the window shade. Simultaneously she brought the salad to the table in a fluted green ceramic bowl, tossed the gleaming greens with two wooden spoons, and left the bowl where it was. Around it she arranged two baskets of freshly sliced French bread, a platter of several pâtés, a grand and hearty looking guacamole, an almond cake, and the truffles. Mary Frances began telling some story about the Concord grape jam, which I could not locate anywhere on the table, though maybe she could. Not that it mattered.

"The process of making it is so time-consuming: you have to work through piles and piles of grape skins and grape seeds, and then you end up with only two small jars of jam. The first time I made it, I said, 'Never again.' So the next year I suggested that Noni do it, which she did."

Norah glanced up from the chopping block in the kitchen, the memory all too evident in her forced smile. Undaunted, the older sister forged ahead.

"But then Noni also vowed 'Never again,' so the next year I was back at it myself, skins and all. By now," she summed up, "Noni has done it two years in a row because I had my hip replacement. Now I told Noni when she has her hip replacement, I'll do it two years in a row."

Norah's expression at that moment took me back to Saturday-afternoon Laurel and Hardy movies, when Olly would shake his head and say to Stan, "This is another fine mess you've gotten me into." Norah is the reality side of the team; Mary Frances, the fantasy. Norah looks directly at things with her laser-straight gaze, while her sister's eyes dart around for fascinating details, whether or not they're there. Norah speaks nothing but the truth; Mary Frances is always transforming it into art. But they both hold their own, and one way or the other the Concord grape jam will probably get made.

Norah made no comment, so Peter and I tried to shift

the conversation to less sticky topics, like what Norah does for a living.

"I'm a psychiatric social worker," she said, a comfortable smile returning to her kind, strong face. "Mary Frances always likes to say I'm a psychiatrist, but, well, you know how Mary Frances exaggerates here and there."

I fastened my eyes firmly on the guacamole, which I found less challenging than looking directly at either of the sisters. Peter opted for pursuing the course of Norah's career. She spoke easily and forthrightly of her past. She got her undergraduate degree at the University of Michigan at Ann Arbor, where their uncle had been dean of the law school. But the real reason she went was that "Mother had one of her notions" that she should "go East" to school. When she graduated, in 1939, her mother was ill, so she came home to work with her father on the family newspaper.

"I was the society editor," she announced and, noting our amused reaction, continued to explain. "It was a big job in Whittier. You know, small towns are made up of organizations and auxiliaries and grand exalted rulers. My father felt that these were really a central part of the community. Every single night he was out at one of those things. I had a lot to report on, especially the women's groups: the Lionesses, Women of the Moose, the Rotary Anns."

"I guess that was a time when women did that sort of thing," I suggested.

"They still do!" Norah laughed and then asked

whether I would like some more bread to go with the too-many slices of pâté I had generously served myself. "In Jenner and Guerneville, all around here, it's the same thing."

In the early forties she also worked on a newspaper in Hawaii, where she lived for a while on the island of Molokai with her godmother, Aunt Gwen.

"You know Aunt Gwen," she nodded to me. "MF has written about her."

"Noni could have been a writer, too," Mary Frances added with audible admiration. Like her sister Norah had started writing when quite young. After Mary Frances married and moved to Dijon, she and Norah sent their poems to one another. Despite the difference in their ages, they respected each other as two people of vision who—as Mary Frances wrote to her at the time—"see mice in the sky and gray lace round the moon."

Mary Frances reminded us that Norah wrote several stories in Hawaii and sent them to Katharine White at *The New Yorker.* White was very enthusiastic about them and had just a few suggestions for revisions.

"Katharine wanted me to come to New York and write," Norah explained, "but I didn't want to do that."

Mary Frances didn't do that either, Norah continued, even though it might have been beneficial for her to be around people with similar interests. Her friends said she was isolating herself because of the girls.

"Norah didn't do the revisions," Mary Frances added,

"because she decided she didn't want to be a writer anyway. She wanted to be a psychiatrist."

This remark brought Norah back to the story of her training as a psychiatric social worker, in which she got a master of arts in the early forties from the University of Chicago. There she met and fell in love with John Barr, who was quickly drafted and sent to Fort Sam Houston in Texas. She took a job with the Red Cross in Utah. Their marriage was, in a way, "MF's fault."

"MF went to New York and married Donald Friede. The next thing, I got a postcard from Atlantic City with a nice picture of Doty and Donald. They both looked so triumphant and happy. Anyway Dote wrote on the back: 'Go thou and do likewise.' So I did!" (Dote was Norah's refinement of Doty, an even more intimate version, and obviously even more forbidden to outsiders).

Mary Frances began to tease her sister about a psychiatrist with whom Norah had studied years ago, the man who psychoanalyzed her as part of her training. Norah didn't think it was so funny, nor did she like the idea that Mary Frances uses the eminent man's name, Dr. Sheehy, as a nickname for her cat. And when Norah is not smiling, she looks very, very stern, sterner than most.

But a moment later both were laughing about the time they stayed at a luxury hotel in Los Angeles, guests of the *Los Angeles Times*, which was presenting an award to M. F. K. Fisher.

As Mary Frances explained it, they went "to see some

old friends and do a trained-seal act at the *LA Times*. Norah and I went VIP, but I well know there is no such thing as a free lunch and was prepared to keep a straight face and say 'thank you' on cue."

Speaking of faces reminded Mary Frances of the time she and Norah were in Marseille and she fell smack on her face. "I had two black eyes for almost three weeks! (There I go boasting again.) Of course I had a broken nose, too, which for about ten days looked more like a stepped-on ripe fig than a human proboscis, and I also had eight or ten stitches on my forehead in what is now a nice vertical frown above and between my eyebrows. But it was those strange, bloodshot eyes looking from deep purple-black pits that really got to me. As I remember, I did not hurt at all. I really felt sorry for poor Noni," she added, looking over at her. "She had to look at me all day."

Fortunately Norah had other things to do during that trip. She was very interested in Mary Magdalene at the time.

"Noni spent hours searching for information and old good stories, apocryphal or otherwise, while I wandered around the old port. It was a good trip though."

"You must have learned quite a bit about Mary Magdalene during that trip," I said, looking directly at Mary Frances.

"Oh, no. Noni's the expert, aren't you, Noni?"

Norah nodded and cut the almond cake and opened the box of truffles. She didn't ask "which" or anything difficult like that. She could tell by looking at us that we had no intention of discriminating between the options. Maybe it's her professional training, or maybe she just knows two gluttons when she sees them. She left the cake knife in place so we could serve ourselves.

As we neared the bottom of the sauvignon blanc, I became emboldened enough to ask, "And what happens when you are angry with each other?"

They looked at each other, the family resemblance more obvious from this angle; their profiles could be two sides of the same face. Neither of them smiled from embarrassment, nor did they seem to mind the question. Mary Frances arched her eyebrows the slightest bit and said, "We get very polite."

The Unexpected Host

"Who is it?" she called out when I knocked on the door.

It was a fair question, a question anyone whose door is knocked upon has a right to ask. For most people it's a way of finding out who is on their door's other side. But with Mary Frances I wasn't sure that's what she meant. I was afraid what she meant was something like, "Go away; I'm not expecting anyone."

She should have been expecting someone—us, to be specific. After all, she had invited the three of us for lunch that Wednesday noon, and we had just finished driving the two hours to get there by the appointed hour. Could she have forgotten?

Of course the drive from San Francisco into the wine country is a beautiful two hours, whether or not there's a destiny at the other end: hills capped with chartreuse crew cuts, puffs of friendly fog, and, this time, an unfamiliar stand of cypress trees that we passed, first on our right and then on our left, and then we realized we were lost. It took only seconds to get back on the road, but it was long enough for one of those insoluble spats about who was the last one to take the map out of the car. This led to mutual reprimands to "put things back from now on" and to the usual muttering finale about consistency being the "hobgoblin of little minds."

What all this meant, getting lost and all, though we didn't want to admit it, was that we were a little nervous because of Matthew. This was the first time we had brought him along on one of these lunches so precious to us. We just wanted everything to go well, to work the way it always worked with her: like a crescendo, so that at the very high point of our visit, when everything was exhilaratingly intimate and absurd and funny, we would be walking out the door. We must come up again soon, we would be vowing breathlessly, hugging and leaving at the same time, not unmindful of the Golden Gate Bridge traffic down the road apiece. Everybody promised. Soon.

It was never soon, of course. There were always a few letters, phone calls, uncooperative schedules in between. But finally we had worked it out for December 28; it was just a coincidence that Matthew was around. Usually he's at school in London. He lives there with his mother, Peter's former wife, and spends his vacations with us. We asked Mary Frances whether it was all right if we brought him along, and she said, of course; she liked a good British accent around the house. She wanted to know if English schoolboys eat as many cookies as Americans. A few days later she called back.

"Was that the twenty-eighth or the thirty-first for our lunch?" she asked. She hadn't had her appointment book by her side the other day.

"The twenty-eighth," I reminded her.

"Oh, thank goodness. That's just fine, then." She sighed in obvious relief.

As we drove into her driveway, the cows were out in force. These cows, I had noticed on a few previous occasions, projected only two attitudes. Either they looked up at you as if you didn't belong; or they looked *away* from you as if you didn't belong. In either case they managed to communicate a certain bovine lack of cordiality.

Maybe that's why I was so alert to that uncertain tone I thought I was hearing now in response to my knock at the door. But I just gritted my teeth, cleared my throat and called in through the crack in the door.

"It's me-Peter-and-Matthew," I answered, trying to hide in the crowd verbally.

"Me-Peter-and-Matthew!?" she repeated.

Was she saying "Wow! Terrific! Finally!" Or was she saying "Really? Aren't you three days early, dear?"

One thing I was sure of: she had invited us for the twenty-eighth. But if she thought otherwise and was not expecting us for lunch today, it wasn't going to make any difference. Even if I were right, what did it matter? It was one of those times one might as well be wrong; I would tell her she was probably right anyway, and I was probably wrong; my calendar is such a total disaster—I would elaborate to reinforce just how wrong I was—it's like a land mine: you touch one date and another date explodes. It's no wonder I got confused, I would say, apologizing, backing out the door. We'll just be on our merry way. Goodbye, now; talk to you in a few days when I get my silly old calendar straightened out.

Meanwhile Matthew pulled at his tie as if he strongly regretted his early-morning decision to wear one. He was staring at the huge table, the length and breadth of a Ping-Pong table, which filled almost the whole porch outside the front door. It was covered with potted geraniums, armsful of newspaper-wrapped calla lilies, clusters of tarragon and thyme, a pot full of fat, yellow tomatoes. People were always bringing her significant portions of their gardens: there were lemons, several varieties, unusual lettuces in all colors, scatterings of unnamed herbs, and, in the interstices, the stems of things long since plucked free from their roots. But what got Matthew's attention were the four plump-bodied, satiny eggplants. Why would anyone want even one eggplant, he was asking me with his eyes, much less a quartet. Underneath it all maybe there was a Ping-Pong table, underneath the layers of new interests and changing concerns that, by now, supplanted anything like Ping-Pong in her life.

Peter was reaching for something on the far corner of the table. "This looks fresh." He smiled, handing it to me. It was the day's newspaper. At least I thought it was. I could not read the date; I couldn't read anything but the name, in fact: *The Armenian Daily News.*

Well, I thought, pushing the door open another eighth

of an inch, we could always pretend we were just dropping by to deliver the newspaper.

"So, what are you all standing out there for? Come in! Come in!" Her voice was strong, demanding, actually. It caught me off guard, so immersed was I in formulating contingency plans, a graceful exit, if it came to that. Peter and Matthew didn't seem concerned one way or the other. They were yards ahead of me already, clicking along the black tiled hallway, down the three slick black steps, and into the big living room–dining room–kitchen–office.

She was standing in front of the sink, surrounded by herb vinegars in progress, arranging red peppers on a little wrought-iron tree that seemed, strangely enough, made for that purpose. She was smiling like crazy.

"Oh, this must be Matthew," she said brightly, a verbal red carpet filling the space between us. "How nice to meet you."

That was convincing. She must have expected us; she certainly sounded as if she expected Matt, with his name at the tip of her tongue and all that. But as we walked toward her, feeling sublimely welcomed, I couldn't help noticing the table.

It was stacked with books, half-scribbled-on notepads, magazines with place marks in them: the signs of writing going on? If she was writing, she didn't need to eat, at least not in any organized way, not like a human being. I knew that much about writing.

"You caught me off guard, a little." She was incredibly composed at this intrusion, if indeed it was an intrusion. "I had to go to town unexpectedly this morning. I just got back."

There wasn't a stick of food in sight.

"I haven't even had a chance to make a fire."

Maybe it was in the refrigerator, all made. I didn't think so. You can tell when a house has food in it, all made. It's not the cooking smells or anything; it happens even when the meal is not yet put together, or was cooked ahead, yesterday. A house that's waiting to feed you is a charged environment. It ticks.

I couldn't hear any ticking, but I did see that there were two packages behind her, wrapped in orange-colored butcher paper. Was that it? Shrimp or something? At that moment she turned aside and, in less than an instant, packed the two parcels quickly and eternally into the freezer. Maybe they were ticking after all, but not for us.

"There" is all she said.

She didn't exactly look calm; she looked radiant, glowing in her blue and white striped smock, African style, like the dashikis I used to sew for all the men I thought I cared about at one time, none of whom deserved them now that I think of it. But the airy, clear-sky colors of the smock made it Irish, made her Irish, even more than she is. She was hugging us with specific hugs, one and all. I handed her *The Armenian Daily News*.

"Oh, yes. My subscription. When that story I wrote about my Armenian rug man appeared, they made me an honorary Armenian. They make sure I get the paper and everything."

She was bustling us over to the fireplace, damning the drizzling day not so much for being sloshy and cold but for being unseasonable. "We don't have this weather at this time of year. It's just silly, that's all." She put her arm on Matthew's shoulder. "I guess your English weather is worse though, Matthew?"

He was enchanted with her already. Not that he said anything much. But he smiled the way fourteen-year-olds smile when they're trying to protect their private hideouts but can't help letting you know they're in there.

"Much worse," he said to make her happy.

He and Peter started to help stack wood in the iron fireplace, but she kept calling them off, insisting on doing it all herself. Somehow at the same time she was offering us everything from ginger beer to white wine. Soon it felt very comfortable, the crackling wood, the green singing flames. She knew what she was doing, whatever she was doing. Her next question made me realize that it was I who didn't know what we were doing, especially about lunch.

"And what are your plans?" she asked Matt sweetly, actually more flirtatious than sweet.

Plans? What did she mean by plans? Real plans, like for lunch this afternoon? Or less relevant material, like what he might be thinking about doing for the rest of his life?

Matthew started telling her about his O levels and A levels and other English educational enigmas. We all chimed in to condemn the British use of the term *public school* for "private school" and vice versa. We were reminded of the scene in Hitchcock's *The Lady Vanishes,* where two Englishmen congratulate each other on being the only two people who stand up reverently during the Hungarian Rhapsody, which, they assure each other, must be the Hungarian national anthem. Matthew then told his Cornish joke about removing half of the brain from the "bloke" from Devon, where they call everybody "me darlin' " and "me 'andsome." Peter expanded the linguistic disapprovals to the French and their use of the word *hôte* to mean both "host" and "guest," a phenomenon he discovered when reading Camus one day, he explained. She charmed Matthew completely, calling him alternately "Yank" or "handsome young Englishman," depending on the drift. She told him her Hollywood story.

"I made fifty bucks a week," she began. "My secretary made three hundred and fifty."

Even more incongruous was what she did there, working for Paramount Pictures.

"I was a gag writer," she said, stopping abruptly to appreciate Matthew's shock at this admission. Those familiar with the absurdity with which she views things like rutabagas or with her subtly sarcastic directions to the novice cook on how to boil water have no trouble seeing the gag writer behind the gourmet. Still, the vision of M. F. K. Fisher scurrying around the likes of Bob Hope, Dorothy Lamour, Bing Crosby . . .

"I wrote for the 'Road' movies, *Road to Rio, Road to* wherever," she explained. One time she was asked to write a gag, and she went straight back to her office and in about three minutes had it all done, got it typed up, and delivered it. To her amazement they told her it was unacceptable and she had to try again. Luckily someone clued her in; the problem was simply that she had done it too fast. She should have written the thing in three minutes but then put it in a drawer for two weeks. At that point it would be welcomed; they might even write a whole movie around it, as long as they thought it took an inordinate length of time.

In her elegantly mischievous way she managed during her short tenure in Hollywood to upset enough apple carts to be banned forever from the celluloid kingdoms, never to darken their tinsel again. Some of the quaint customs she inveighed against were those that prevented writers from negotiating salaries or leaving one studio to write for another.

"And yet a lot of people you wouldn't suspect wrote for Hollywood in those days," she revealed in an enticing tone that kept Matthew interested, whether or not he was familiar with any of the specific names she mentioned. These were legitimate writers whose names, fortunately for their careers, never showed up on the stuff. The Hollywood bosses had everything rewritten by their own people anyway, she said; they thought they were the only ones who could do it right after all. She laughed. She met everybody from Shirley Temple, when she was a child actress, to Hedy Lamarr, who, she explained, spoke no English: she would memorize and recite the script, but basically she had no idea what she was talking about. Mary Frances mentioned Preston Sturges, Ava Gardner,

Greta Garbo, Joseph Cotton, Mackinlay Kantor, and how she would sometimes go on a jaunt with some of them to Mexico for the afternoon.

"Oh, that must have been fun," I chirped in.

"No, not really," she countered. She went on to mention Lillian Hellman, whom Mary Frances described as a person who created such bad vibrations when she walked into a room that people immediately started being nasty to each other.

Mary Frances covered just about every film star I'd ever heard of, and didn't seem to speak too kindly of anyone. In the spirit of mutual calumny, I offered my ill-founded supposition: "Orson Welles must have been awful."

She looked at me for a long second, as if to reprimand me for making slanderous remarks about people I didn't even know. "No. He was very nice, in fact. Perhaps it was the roles he played in movies that made you think that."

"Yes, I suppose he was so good at being evil he fooled everybody. Sure fooled me," I added with a tinny, false-sounding chuckle that she, mercifully, pretended not to notice.

"The best part of that job," she confessed, "was that I had to watch movies for hours on end."

Matthew smiled at the vision of such idyllic work and told her he'd always wanted to be a stuntman. Peter cringed for a moment—he had convinced himself that Matt had outgrown this ambition—but basically we all felt warm and giggly and witty.

We were not, however, eating lunch.

For a moment I was stunned by the horrifying thought that she had expected me to bring lunch that day. Not that I would have minded; I had done that several times. But when our signals got crossed, it was always disastrous. Whenever I brought lunch on a day she had made lunch—or didn't bring lunch on a day she had expected me to—the silences that ensued were the longest in the history of gastronomy. Brillat-Savarin must have reserved his worst condemnations for those who brought unexpectedly, or who did not bring when they were expected to.

"And she brought this whole meal *unannounced,*" she once told me about an otherwise nice enough visitor of hers. The unannounced meal is not worth bringing, I noted to myself that day.

I tried to dismiss these bothersome thoughts and concentrated on convincing myself that she thought we were just stopping by for a visit, and consequently she was not the least bit concerned about lunch. She might well think we were taking Matt around Sonoma and into the wine country, a little California culture on his vacation. But once I realized this, or thought I realized it, I wanted to get us all out of there without causing anybody any embarrassment. I had an immediate impulse to hide the basketful of pumpkin muffins I had brought as my contribution to the meal that we weren't going to have. But I couldn't very well shove a dozen muffins under my shirt. A little New Year's gift, I would tell her. It was that time of year, fortunately. I thought I'd let a little time go by, and then I'd ask her if she knew any good places for lunch around there.

"I've been reading about an awful lot of restaurants up here," I began, not wanting to be too direct. "Seems like there's a new one every day."

"I don't pay much attention to that sort of thing, you know," she responded, resuming her conversation with Peter about his book on the seventies. I waited.

"I suppose the old places are the best," I began again haltingly.

"Well, I don't know what old places you're talking about. But if I were looking for something to eat around here, I suppose I would just go down to that broken-down diner in town. They aren't sophisticated enough to do anything but make their own soup. But I'd eat the packaged crackers that come with it, not their bread. The bread's awful. So's everything else. It's all from central supply, you know."

Well so much for radicchio salads with warm Sonoma goat cheese.

"So you'd go right down there for lunch?"

"Me? No. I wouldn't go anywhere. I'd have my lunch right here."

Actually I didn't care about restaurant recommendations; I just wanted to introduce the fact that we had not come for lunch (even though we had) and that we had plans to go elsewhere (even though we hadn't). There was something exquisitely subtle about all this. I wasn't sure anyone was getting it. I looked at Matthew, who seemed to be listening more intently to his father than is his wont. Either he's trying to forget he's starving, or he's become fascinated by the seventies all of a sudden. A few more minutes and I'll gracefully engineer our exit. I had it under control, more or less.

"Well this has been very lovely," I began, clearing my throat in the unmistakable body language of departure. I tried to catch Peter's eye so he could see that I was attempting to get us out of there, even though he wouldn't know why. In cases of extreme emergency, like this one, we had an uncanny ability to communicate nonverbally. If I could just wink at him or something, he would know that whatever harebrained unexpectedness had come over me, he should ask about it later.

But Peter was paying no attention. In fact, he was blissfully and completely comfortable, as was Matt. By contrast, I was in a state of almost perpetual motion, alternately clearing my throat, shifting in my chair, and winking. No one noticed except possibly Mary Frances, who was looking at me strangely.

"Yes," she answered. "It has been lovely. But now you're getting hungry, is that it? Well you're right, of course. I'd better get on with our lunch. You certainly come right to the point, don't you, dear?" She looked over at Peter for corroboration: "Nothing subtle about her, is there?"

Before long she was assembling a crispy, cheese-topped pasta dish, popping it into the oven, taking it out.

She removed from the back of the fridge a plastic container full of zucchini marinating.

The freezer was full of half loaves of the Sonoma French Bakery's caraway sourdough, one of which she had popped into the oven to defrost. When she checked the loaf it was still frozen, so she filled her breadbasket with my pumpkin muffins and some grainy wheat rolls. Nothing had been made ahead, but it didn't matter; she obviously was prepared for us today, lunch and all. Or was she?

I still wasn't sure. At any rate, she pulled it off, lived up to her own translation of Brillat-Savarin's dictum: "To invite people to dine with us is to make ourselves responsible for their well-being for as long as they are under our roofs."

As we were leaving, I said, choosing my words deliberately, "You did a beautiful job."

"Oh, no." She creased her eyes at me. Did she know that I was on to her, or *was* I on to her? Or was she on to me? "You're the one who did the beautiful job." She looked me straight in the eyes. "Those tiny little muffins made the meal," she said.

Gable and Leigh
and Fisher:

Just Us
Chickens

I didn't know the phone was going to ring when I started making the *sfinciuni*. If I had had a suspicion that Mary Frances was going to call, I wouldn't have got myself involved with this sticky, pizza-like bread dough in the first place. I was making it to bring up to her place for our lunch together, the three of us—"just us chickens," as she put it when she invited Peter and me to lunch.

"What about my boyfriend Peter?" she had asked. "Will he be coming with you?"

Her "boyfriend Peter" was the same person she also called "your boyfriend Peter," depending on how playful and chummy she was feeling, and how proprietary. Peter and I had been living together for thirteen years, and our daughter, Natasha, was then five years old. Because of baby-sitting and deadlines and the general state of improbability that obtains with two writers in one household,

Peter and I didn't always visit Mary Frances together. Quite often we just couldn't arrange it.

But it was always fun when we did, especially because she liked Peter so much. He was down-to-earth, had no pretensions and was angry, elated and irreverent about the same things that made her angry, elated and irreverent. With his historian's breadth of knowledge, he often seemed to know more about her life and times than he'd actually been through. It made them kindred and it made her laugh. She identified with the iconoclast in him. The incident that cemented their friendship occurred at a gathering in a huge San Francisco hotel ballroom—actually the most opulent book party I'd ever seen. Mary Frances, who was seated in a wheelchair, was greeting the line of people queued up near her. Despite her smiles and friendly hand shaking, she looked more than mildly uncomfortable, and every time the line thinned out, she quickly turned the wheelchair and tried to scurry away before anyone noticed.

"I'd like to talk to Craig," she'd whisper, and Peter or I would guide her over to wherever Mr. Claiborne was standing, also surrounded by admirers. They would speak for a few minutes, but soon they would have to tend to their respective queues, their conversation hopelessly interrupted by well-wishers. In the background someone with a microphone was referring to Mary Frances in such terms as the *"bonne femme* of American cuisine" and making champagne toasts to food and wine and art and how none of it would be the same without M. F. K. Fisher. Her face brightened to its proper pinkness only once during the ceremony, when Peter bent down and whispered in her ear, "Don't you think this is all bullshit?"

She loved it: her eyes sparkled, her smile released into a real laugh. It was exactly what she wanted to hear, providing scatological balance to otherwise elegant circumstances. In fact, right after that she left, liberated by the fact that someone she respected could so summarily dismiss the proceedings.

It was this down-to-earthness that made me think that *sfinciuni* would be the perfect food for "us chickens." Its very simplicity, the minimal number of ingredients (a little yeast and olive oil, some semolina mixed into the flour, if you have it) would appeal to her. That and the fact that it takes forever to make. I didn't really have the time. "And if you cannot rightly find [the time]," she had written in *How to Cook a Wolf*, "make it, for probably there is no chiropractic treatment, no Yoga exercise, no hour of meditation in a music-throbbing chapel, that will leave you emptier of bad thoughts than this homely ceremony of making bread." OK already.

I thought of these words several times as I slapped the dough around on the marble slab, doubting that the rumpled, straggly mass before me would ever turn into anything. But once I got its attention, it started to become very much its own person. By the time I was ready to cover it with a damp cloth, it had developed the presence of an Italian boxer—Rocky Marciano was the name that came to mind—over whose shoulders I was draping a towel. By that

time I had become a mere helper in the process of forming
this dough into the two-crusted tomato-and-cheese-filled
pie that would look, when I finished, probably much like
an introverted pizza. But I did not finish, because the phone
rang.

"Don't come up after all" was the gist of it. She had
hurt her foot, and the doctor told her if she didn't stay off
it, she would be in the hospital for three days.

"But come up anyway" was her almost immediate
amendment. "Maybe you can come by for an aperitif," she
said, her voice rising on the final syllable, to make it obvious that she realized the absurdity of using a word like
aperitif with the likes of us. "Anyway, I'd like you both to
have lunch somewhere. On me. My treat. I may not be able
to feed you here, but I can get you some good food. Some
food, anyway. I don't know how good it will be. Can you
do it? What does Peter say?"

Driving from our place to hers was a spectator sport
with a front-row view of eucalyptus trees, cow-covered
fields, and villa-esque wineries. Even the cemetery in Terra
Linda, with its cloud-white tombstones and green suede
slopes, appeared inviting from the highway. And often
there were a few surprised goats and clumps of tipsy cypress trees to look forward to. Glen Ellen itself is a tumble
of strawberry-blond hills trimmed with red bottlebrush
and a distant fleece of evergreens. The road interrupts what
would otherwise be an endless meadow of long grasses the
color of bamboo and rust and unripe olives. Patches of
orange poppies show up at their whim, the perfect state

flower for a place with the same unpredictable tendencies. The ride there was restful and always worth it when we spent the afternoon jabbering away with Mary Frances. But to drive that distance and not see much of her was another story.

Still, there were three temptations: it was a beautiful morning; we could at least drop by for a short visit; and we already had a baby-sitter for the day. That probably was the deciding factor. That and the opportunity of stuffing Rocky in the freezer. "What the hell. Let's go" is what Peter said.

When we arrived, there were no cars outside, the gate was shut, and the door appeared to be locked.

"This reminds me of last time," Peter said with a worried purse of the lips.

"Yes, I wonder . . . ," I replied, remembering the similar ominous silence that greeted us at our previous visit a few months ago. We had just finished unloading the various lunch accoutrements and piling them into each other's arms. When we reached the door, it suddenly opened, apparently of its own volition. Standing there were a man and a woman who looked like professional evictors. They had long, straw-colored faces, gloomy eyes, and a set of keys.

"Mrs. Fisher isn't here," they said, in a low-droned duet. "She's in the hospital."

They let some silence intervene, too much for comfort. But the moment was theirs; we could only wait for them to continue.

"Nothing serious," the woman said finally, mumbling about a hurt hip. "Mrs. Fisher asked us to call everyone in her appointment book. But you people didn't answer. You must have left hours ago."

We asked if we could visit Mary Frances in the hospital or at least call her. But the woman kept reassuring us that "Mrs. Fisher is fine" and that "she'll be calling you herself in a few days." I looked down at my tray of something called triple-nut treats; I had baked them just before we left, and they were still warm. I didn't know whether Mary Frances would like them, but I did know that the name would make her wince, and I had been looking forward to that all morning. I handed the tray to the dour twosome.

"Could you give these goodies to Mrs. Fisher, please? I know she hates hospital food."

But they shook their heads in unison, saying that she would get "plenty to eat," as if that were the solution instead of the problem.

As soon as we were certain that we really didn't have to worry about Mary Frances, we began to feel sorry for ourselves. We felt that we had lost a day, a day that, as we drove back past the almost motionless black and white cows cluttering her driveway, was dazzling and dancing around us. Fortunately we saw it in time for what it could be, an afternoon of free wandering in the nearby Valley of the

Moon, finding the site of Jack London's Wolf House, built to last a thousand years but burned down to the ground before it was finished.

Shortly thereafter our nonchalant sense of direction was to lead us to the Glen Ellen Winery, where we tasted the very Chardonnay Mary Frances so often served at lunch. Being practical minded, we decided to buy a few extra bottles, because, we thought, it would be less expensive at the winery. Instead, we came away with some special expensive Chardonnay that was, we were told, sold only at the winery; "not available in stores" was how they put it. Why we did that we really never understood. It is part of the mystique of the wine country: ordinarily rational people find themselves on a winery tour and suddenly begin to believe that there is some reality to be found in concepts like "tannic finish" and "vegetal edge." They stop laughing at phrases like "grass and coffee in the nose." They think they see a relationship between the logical and the enological. At least that's what happened to us as our keenly cultivated sales resistance vaporized into a mist of rationalizations. Oh, of course it was a better wine and all that. But the farther away we got from the winery, the less we were able to convince ourselves. Nevertheless, we had no trouble drinking this generally unavailable wine later that night, along with the entire tray of triple-nut treats.

Today as we headed toward the front door, I kept expecting it to be opened by those same little gnomes of our prior visit. The silence was disturbing, but it wasn't the absence of noise that seemed so strange. It was that the smell of wonderful things cooking, or just cooked, wasn't drifting out into the yard. We tried the door. It opened into a suspiciously odorless quiet.

"Mary Frances," I called.

"Come into the bedroom, dearies," she sang out, strong-voiced and cheery from somewhere to the left of the doorway. We stepped into a room full of bookshelves and tables and in-baskets, trays of typewritten pages and letters, advance copies of books, and bound galleys of books-to-be. Sitting on a chair was a painting, very flaked and chipped, that looked strangely familiar. A woman? Yes. It was, I finally realized, the painting on the cover of her book *Sister Age.* She must keep it here in the bedroom. Usually she greeted us in the other room, an everything-in-one space crammed with the papers, letters, and magazines that had obviously been carted into her bedroom. As we stepped in, it looked nothing like a bedroom. Except that beyond and above the stacks and piles was an enormous bed with Mary Frances in it, facing all this work.

She looked terrific. She was beaming, aglow in a bright Prussian blue something-or-other, more a dressy evening outfit than anything resembling pajamas. Into her fluffed and silky hair she had nestled a barrette of the same blue color. She had not neglected her eyebrows, which arched mischievously when she widened her dancing gray eyes at us and just as mischievously when she didn't. We were both relieved to see her looking so great, better than we'd seen her in a long time.

"Kisses, kisses," she ordered, her hands chirping open and closed like a big bird's beak. "Come, come."

She didn't want us to feel uncomfortable about entering her bedroom, invading her private sleeping chambers like this; but we did, not so much because it was her bedroom but because it was her work space. We knew how vital her work was to her, more so even than her sleep. She didn't complain about insomnia, though I had noticed lately that she often had tales to tell about the nether regions of 4:00 A.M. radio talk shows. In the morning, however, she'd be ready, somehow, for her daily parade of visitors.

Her calendar was scribbled over with recognizable names: Miriam Ungerer, Wilfrid Sheed, Betty Fussell, James Villas, Maya Angelou, Raymond Sokolov, a princess, an ambassador, writers and photographers for *Town & Country, Bon Appetit, House & Garden, Modern Maturity, Newsday, The New York Times, PBS*. Many visitors were complete strangers to her. But they were would-be friends, people who had read her books and wrote of their admiration, expecting nothing and receiving, instead, an invitation to lunch. When she was interviewed in San Francisco's Herbst Theater before a capacity crowd of several hundred, one overly enthusiastic person asked her, during the question-and-answer period, for her address. People were shocked that Mary Frances gave it out without hesitation. She thought nothing of it.

"Hell, if someone wants to write and say, 'My mother died yesterday and reading you made me feel better'—and that's the type of letter I usually receive—then why not?" she told me. But now she was in the midst of a spate of out-of-towners, people coming to California for food conventions or writers' conferences. They flew into San Francisco Airport from New York or Washington, D.C., assuming that everything must be near the airport and discovering that not even San Francisco was near the airport, never mind Glen Ellen. So they were always renting cars and driving hours and hours and calling, lost, from Jack London's Wolf House or from the piroshki factory just down the road. And so when they finally showed up, she didn't have the heart to tell these poor, frazzled, jet-lagged admirers that she was in the middle of writing an article so could they please make it snappy. She sat there listening and giving them bits of life, hers and everybody's. I think she put up with these pilgrimages because they gave her a way of enjoying things vicariously, unless the conversation turned completely useless. Only then did she become contrary, not her usual contrary, which had a certain charm to it, but quite contrary, Mary, Mary.

"She suffers no fools," a long-time friend said about her, someone who felt that Mary Frances was too selective and would not waste her time with the virtuosos of idle chatter. That may have been true once, perhaps when she was still able to drive and could go wherever she wanted. But here in Glen Ellen, far from the main roads—socially, psychologically as well as geographically—she seemed willing to grant an audience to anyone who had the temerity to ask. It is her means of getting around.

On one of our recent visits, she was besieged by a twosome who was "into wine." In fact, they were into her wine, or at least into her refrigerator, from which they kept extracting bottles of various vintages. The woman had brought snail eggs and trout caviar, which she kept arranging decoratively in baskets of flowers. She would then take pictures of everything before she served it. The two were also "into lace" and gold-sequined silk and other semiprecious fluff they had just brought back from Venice or somewhere. As they unwrapped tissue-papered parcels of their treasures, they explained that they were going to have them made into collars and sashes as soon as they found an artisan skilled enough—"you just can't find people these days who know how to do this kind of work." The woman passed along wads of this gossamer to Mary Frances, who fingered it politely and smiled and told about beautiful collars, her own grandmother's, I think she said. These people were only encouraged by her reaction, convinced that they must be utterly fascinating creatures or she wouldn't be spending her time with them. Anyway, that was the day Mary Frances said, as we left while another round of lace was being unparceled for appreciation, "Next time it will be just us chickens."

And this time she was fairly clucking as we chickens walked in; she looked like relief incarnate. Her hurt foot had given her a chance to cancel without guilt a few daysful of admirers. As I pulled her shoulders together in a hug, she felt substantial and healthy, though she looked like a fragile, preened bird perched among the quilted cumulous billowings of her comforter. As soon as I saw the full extent of her eyebrows, I was reassured. I knew if her eyebrows were up, she was up.

Also, she was up to something, fluttering away in her feathery coverings as she asked calm-sounding questions that she couldn't wait to get over with. Finally finished with these prerequisites, she got to the point.

"Why don't you go out to the kitchen, dear," she began, obviously planning to unpack her mysteries word by word,

"and"—one finger in the air flicking me in the right direction, as if I may have forgotten where the kitchen was—

"next to the refrigerator you'll find three glasses and an envelope . . ." a pause totally for effect,

"and"—more fingers up in the air, making a shape—

"open the refrigerator, and you'll find a bottle,"—a bottle shape, that was it—

"of Domaine Chandon champagne. Or sparkling wine, rather. We're supposed to call it sparkling wine now, you know?" she corrected with measured sarcasm.

I found the champagne accompanied by a peach-colored envelope. On it she had written our names in brown Pentel pen followed by the date: "7. XI. 85," the European way she wrote dates. I brought the whole lot in on a tray, and we opened the envelope and the champagne, though not necessarily in that order.

"Did you do all this with your hurt foot?" I asked. She bobbled her head from side to side, as if to shake off any vestiges of unmerited virtue.

"I didn't have much choice in the matter," she answered in a partial mumble, adding, grudgingly, that someone had come by earlier to help out, "not that I needed it."

I opened the envelope. The front of the enclosed card was a reproduction of a movie poster proclaiming, in flame-orange letters, "GONE WITH THE WIND." Next to this was a romantic rendering of Clark Gable looking adoringly down into Vivien Leigh's sultry, half-closed eyes, these popular American lovers locked for all eternity over the tag line "A DAVID O. SELZNICK PRODUCTION." Inside the card was written, in the same brown Pentel as on the envelope, "and *bon appétit!!*" Something fell out and was swallowed immediately by the devouring bed linens.

"Reminded me of you two," she said, smiling and trying to make us feel self-conscious, and succeeding. We had to tell her, at that point, that we had more of a Ralph-and-Alice vision of our relationship.

"You remember? From 'The Honeymooners'?" Peter explained. "Jackie Gleason and Audrey Meadows?"

"Oh, television," she said with disdain. "Don't have one. Wouldn't have one. Never."

I told her she didn't have to worry about Ralph and Alice. They hadn't been on television for thirty years except for the occasional rerun. Thus assured that we had no evil intentions of introducing her to the horrors of TV sitcoms, past or present, she became interested.

"They were from Brooklyn, like me," I explained. "They had a scrungy little apartment with a pan under the icebox. He was a bus driver, Everyman-style, and neither of them had any pretensions: they didn't drink aperitifs or anything. He was always thinking up some futile scheme for making them a fortune, and she was the unwavering voice of reason. He would hitch his bus to a star, and she would take care of the real world until, and after, everything came crashing down. They loved each other, so it was all right if he called her mother a blabbermouth and she said it was stupid for him to go hunting with his fellow members of the Royal Order of the Raccoons, and they often yelled at each other. Not that Peter and I yell at each other," I protested, suddenly self-conscious, "but you know what I mean."

She laughed as she spoke. "I remember something about it. That's how you see each other?" she addressed Peter.

"Frankly, my dear," he said, taking on the role she had assigned, "I don't give a damn."

"Frankly, *my* dear," she countered, bunching up her mouth, "I'd rather think of you as Clark and Vivien, Rhett and Scarlett, not these Ralph and Alice people."

Actually I was getting the Freudian notion that it was herself she saw as Scarlett, scarlet the letter as well as Scarlett-cum-Rhett. Naughty, either way. I was wondering if Peter was her Rhett, just for the moment anyway, just while it lasted, the champagne and everything. It was a little crazy, but she did have this strong attraction to men, an attraction that was, in every case that I had seen, mutual.

It wasn't simply that she was "an outrageous flirt," as one man described her. She once wrote, "I have always held the insufferably smug opinion that if I want a man to love me, he will." But she was able to command a whole roomful of attention, men, women, mixed or matched, if she so chose. There was a sensuality about her, an animal magnetism, a 360-degree alertness. She saw things and felt things and pointed them out like someone turning all the lights on in the room as you walk around. People were attracted to her high sense of life, her wired sensitivity; it could be frantic or silent, sacred, lusty, noble, or each of these in turn.

A woman who had once visited Mary Frances recalled the moment she walked into the house, with the silvery afternoon sun flickering across the couch Mary Frances was sitting on. "She didn't move. She wasn't doing anything, just sitting there. The light was especially beautiful, and she let it run off her face and hands. I thought it was one of the most voluptuous moments of my life. Not sexual; well, maybe it was sexual. I suppose it was in a way. But I always remember it as a wonderfully sensual experience."

Another woman told me that the first time she and her husband visited, Mary Frances told her to lie down in the bathtub! "She said I could see the paintings better that way," she recounted. "So I did! It was an amazing experience, especially because I discovered there a painting by someone I knew. Mary Frances is such a sensual woman, a woman who loves food, loves life. The only problem was that her cat jumped all over me when I climbed into the tub. Maybe she was jealous."

What I had really wanted to ask was what Mary Frances and the woman's husband were doing while she was in the tub. But I didn't.

Peter was pouring the last of the sparkling wine, and we toasted our lunch-to-be.

"I think we should be moving along anyway," I suggested, "me and Ralph."

"Don't you leave this here," she said sternly, picking up the debris that had fallen out of the card into the blankets. They were two crisp, new twenty-dollar bills. We said we were not going to take them, and she said yes, we were, that she was not having us drive all that way without giving us a meal.

"Now what do you feel like eating?"

We didn't really care, we said. But what kind of an answer was that? she asked; of course we cared, and had we ever been to Sharyl's, on the square in Sonoma? she persisted. It wasn't too bad, as restaurants went in the area, none of them being so great as the food writers and travel magazines wanted to make you think they were, but she could call ahead if we'd like. She knew them.

No, we said, no, thank you. We'd rather follow our instincts; see what struck us. It felt freer that way, more adventurous. She gave us a loaf of the Sonoma French Bakery's caraway sourdough that she had "no use for." We said good-bye, all of us happy to have spent time together and to still have time for ourselves. Happy to get rid of us, I thought, and why not? Otherwise she would have no time for her work.

As we drove out the driveway, the red and yellow grapevines looked crisp and alert, enjoying the playful ticklings of the wily Sonoma sun, bright yet autumnal. We turned left onto the highway, full of plans, possibility. A strong primal desire was palpatating in the air between us, the basic human urge for cheese and wine that we could pair up with our inherited sourdough, go find a hill somewhere and make believe we were in Arles or Aix-en-Provence. We passed the piroshki factory and then we passed Sharyl's. It looked like a fortress, with high, thick walls, eggshell-white and trickled with emerald climbing vines. Through a half-closed gate we could see an inner patio, cool and green, wrought-iron and glass, European and Californian.

"What the hell?" is what Peter said; "might as well look at the menu."

First we were reading, and soon therafter, eating coq au vin with roasted red peppers, scallops in white wine, fruit in raspberry sauce with homemade ice cream. Were they being especially attentive? we wondered. Had Mary Frances called after all? She could have; it would not be uncharacteristic of her to advise them that two of her friends might be stopping by. We started to speculate about how she might have described us.

"Gable and Leigh?" Peter suggested, his face full of a sarcastic Gable-like grin.

"Of course," I said as the waiter appeared with some port, compliments of the management. "How else would they have recognized us?"

The Affair:

M. F. K. Fisher and
Brillat-Savarin

Irst I did the arithmetic. M. F. K.
Fisher was in her mid-thirties when she started the translation. She must have been reading, writing, drinking, and
dreaming the man. It's no wonder he captured her heart,
that she fell in love with him "that way": the way you do
when you're married and have two daughters and no time
to carry on an affair properly.

To be honest, this was all my idea, or almost all. She
does admit, in the preface to the translation, that her "love
for the old lawyer burns as brightly as ever." Anyway, I
would ask her all about it. As I drove toward her Glen
Ellen hideaway, I had with me her 1949 translation of *The
Physiology of Taste*, originally written by the French lawyer-
philosopher Jean Anthelme Brillat-Savarin in 1825. But
that particularly happy-looking book, with grapes all over
the cover, was a new edition, recently issued in paperback.

I wasn't sure what she'd say. How do you ask a woman
if she was in love with a man who died nearly a century
before she was born? Some women would find that ridicu-

lous. But not this woman. She's good at falling in love, in all kinds of ways with all kinds of things: people, ideas, moments. That's what her writing is about: enthusiasms. People who think she's a food writer are merely concentrating on one of her enthusiasms. Of course, food writers have a vested interest in trying to make her one of them, so they can plumb her works for paragraphs about tangerines, because they're the best things anybody has ever said about tangerines: sensual, elegant, present. But that's because, underneath it all, she's not talking about tangerines. Her tangerines lie in the subconscious, with all their primal associations intact. She's a thinker, a wanderer, an absorber of life, a philosopher even, but not a food writer. Food writers never quote food writers, anyway: there's the real proof. In fact, the only other person quoted as frequently about food and the art of eating is Brillat-Savarin. And even then it's often Fisher's translation.

Of course, he wasn't a food writer either, I reminded myself; he was a lawyer, a judge, and a raconteur. She assures us, with her wishful use of adjectives, that he was "a tender and sensitive lover" who had "handsome legs." He was also fascinated with every aspect of taste, from its effect on the senses to the niceties of dining. For thirty years he kept notes, almost sub rosa, finally publishing his work with his own funds just before his death. Did he consider his interests inconsistent with his professional status? His translator-friend will know his feelings on the matter. Her research was more than thorough: it was loving, even intimate. In her glosses following the chapters she introduces the reader to bystanders at dinner parties, to the endless odd cousins who proliferated in nineteenth-century Paris, and, most significantly, to Louise, the classic beauty who accommodated Brillat-Savarin's romantic fantasies, in two ways: by having consumption and dying young. Poor Louise was "lost forever when he was only twenty" is how M. F. K. Fisher puts it.

She supplies other background information as well, indulges in more or less relevant speculation ("If he were alive today, he might well be an anesthesiologist"), or just writes whatever she pleases. So it is from these glosses that we learn what Charles Lindbergh ate during his historic transatlantic flight (one and a half sandwiches) and that the French were appalled, if not insulted, that he didn't choose to toast his success with the champagne they had waiting but preferred instead some milk and a roll and a good night's sleep. Another gloss relates how her father's reputation as the family meat carver originated prenuptially with the need to impress his father-in-law-to-be, who considered carving the mark of a true gentleman.

Most of these stories do have their inspiration in the original text, but translators generally do not become so intertwined with their material. Yet it is the glosses that make her *Physiology* as much a contemporary American commentary as it is French and classic. Through them she can converse with her lawyer-lover, dual with him. First he speaks and then, touché, and it's her turn. She can even, if she chooses, ignore him. Her translation is a book within a book, the difference between literal definition and literary dimension.

That always brings up the Edward FitzGerald question: is she translating or paraphrasing? FitzGerald's 1859 translation of the *Rubáiyát of Omar Khayyám* made an exquisite poem in English; so exquisite that it is now considered FitzGerald's own masterpiece, his inspired rendering of the Persian original rather than a true translation. This *Physiology* sounds so much like Mary Frances that I can never help wondering whether she has infused the work with her own style and wit or whether they are there to begin with. Is this book her *Rubáiyát* or his? Even the most faithful translation can transcend the original. With my lapsed French I could tell that hers is not the kind of word-by-word, interlinear translation we performed on Caesar's Gallic wars. His words exuded death and fear, and we worried about whether they were in the ablative case or the nominative of direct address. She was after bigger game.

When I pulled into the long driveway, I saw her standing at the gate. Mary Frances Kennedy Fisher had red lipstick on, and her face was a good pink, with powdery blue eyelids. She was especially pretty that day. Her bright eyes and the wind chimes attacked the air's complacency. She led me out to the porch and set me up, tape recorder and all, making me feel these intrusions were minor, though they were indeed intrusions. I said hello to Mary Jane, who was helping out with the day's chores and at the moment was surrounded by the smell of roasting nuts and burned sugar. I had a thousand questions, but first we talked about *biscotti.*

"Mary Jane and I made this batch of *biscotti* this morning," she announced, pointing to a total of six brittle-looking Italian cookies. Hardly a batch, I said to myself. "But the minute we touched them, they fell apart." Now I noticed the way Mary Jane was standing beside a platter piled with filbert-studded cookie trash: as if she were in mourning.

"What do you think we can do with them?" Mary Frances asked. Was she asking me? I knew better than to answer questions like that. "Do you think they would make a good pie crust or something?" she persisted.

I nodded in a way that would not get me held responsible if things didn't work out for these ill-fated *italiani* the second time round. I tried to change to subject to anything about Jean Anthelme Brillat-Savarin. But the next thing I knew, we were talking about Maurice Chevalier.

"Because I'd done Brillat-Savarin, I was offered a job to translate the life of Maurice Chevalier, called *Mon Paris.* I thought it would be fun to do two Frenchmen."

She tried to capture him as he really was, the man himself, not the Maurice prancing across the screen. She was pleased with the translation. As for him: "He was horrified. He hated it," she said. "He wanted to come across just as he thought people expected, prance and all. He wanted it rewritten so it would be the American image of him: the *gai boulevardier,* the *flâneur.* I didn't do it," she admitted, shrugging her shoulders. "I couldn't do it. I wouldn't do it."

Besides, she was even more excited by another opportunity that followed the appearance of *Physiology*, the prospect of translating the complete works of Colette.

"I've always had enormous respect for her as a writer," she explained. "I thought of spending the rest of my life translating Colette. It's all I would ever have done. But as it turned out, the publishers were only interested in the slightly lascivious, the little innuendos about lesbians and gays, what they considered the dirty parts." So she said, "Absolutely not," and did her own work instead.

Although the publication of *Physiology* did not divert Fisher into a life of translating, it did affect her career immensely. For one thing, prior to publication her literary agent sold a few sections to *Gourmet* magazine. Today this would be considered a coup, a boost to sales. But in her case it was a disaster. *Physiology* was being published by the Limited Editions Club, whose members were paying twenty-five dollars for a boxed, fine-paper edition. An unboxed edition was to be released simultaneously by Heritage Press for five dollars, also a lot of money at the time.

"George Macy, the publisher, was livid," she explained. "He said he was going to lose all his members who wouldn't think of paying twenty-five dollars for something they could read in a magazine. He claimed he lost hundreds of members."

She twisted her mouth into a kind of *c'est la vie* smirk, which disappeared an instant later as she added, "And I lost my agent, Mary Leonard Pritchett. But then I did get Henry Volkening, who was to be my agent for a quarter of a century."

The appearance of *Physiology* had at least one immediate important consequence. When Earle MacAusland, publisher of *Gourmet,* saw it, he said, "This woman's getting too classy for us," and virtually ended the magazine's relationship with her.

"Until then I'd written quite a bit for them. But they only took one or two more pieces after that, . . . one with fine pictures of Marseille, I remember. And that was it."

Strange how one always envisions everyone else's life as a nice, tidy continuum leading from obscurity to renown with very few of the glitches that beset one's own career. Brilliant though this realization may have been, I didn't mention it. I thought of something more relevant: "I understand that with this reprinting of *Physiology* all your works are currently in print for the first time in years."

"Oh, is that right?" she asked, as if this were the sort of thing that meant more to publishers and publicity directors than to writers themselves. At seventy-eight she was working on several articles, one long manuscript, and a "secret project."

I decided to ask her how she got involved in the translation.

"I was horrified at the terrible, terrible translations of Brillat-Savarin. I told Donald Friede, who was my husband at the time, that I could do better, and he said, "Why don't you?" Then he wangled the whole translation deal with

George Macy. It was the largest fee that had ever been paid for a translation. Donald loved to do the biggest and the best, the most puffed up, top-star stuff. Even the illustrations: Pablo Picasso was asked to do them first, but his agent would not let him. Donald was planning to write the great American novel, and I had this job"—she smiled at some vision that was strong enough to make her eyebrows stiffen—"all laid out on that pool table." She continued, explaining how she arranged her work in separate piles across the vast green surface.

"How did you decide what to write for the glosses?" I asked.

"The glosses?" she repeated, as if she was not sure what I was referring to. "Oh, they're very chitchatty. I just did them. I don't remember making any decision at all."

"They fit so well. I wonder what the book would be like if there weren't anything *but* glosses. Do you recall what gave you the idea?"

"Well, frankly, I don't know why I put those in. Probably 'cause I was bored."

I was still wondering what to make of this when Mary Frances got to what was probably her point.

"Tell me when you want some lunch, dear."

"In a few minutes," I said, realizing I'd better get around to the part about whether she was in love with him. I could have asked her directly, but I opted instead for the oblique approach.

"*The Physiology,*" I began, "is such a unique work that it doesn't seem to fit into any category. It's almost a genre in itself. You seem the perfect match for it in that sense, a writer without a real genre to fall into. Do you think that's why you worked so well together, you and Jean Anthelme?"

"I don't know about that," she answered, looking pleased. "But it certainly was fun, and I learned an awful lot—like how to keep everything clear and simple—from his prose. He wrote such beautiful prose. If you followed it, you couldn't go wrong. It's rather like following a recipe by Julia Child: might be boring as hell, but if you actually do it . . ."

Her eye wandered immediately over to the plate of *biscotti* crumbs.

"Yes," I said, turning off the tape. "But then you'll make such a great pie of it all in the end."

The
Fatherland

"Last night I had a dream about robbing a bank," Mary Frances told me one opulently sunny June day as we sat in her suite at the Stanford Court Hotel in San Francisco, surrounded by brocade, velvet, and mahogany. "I know just how I would do it."

She would throw a brick through the window of the bank, she said, her eyes lighting up like a pouncing cat's; but first she would wrap the brick in a cloth so it wouldn't hurt anybody. As she described her MO, complete with details of the getaway, it seemed plausible enough, even though she was sitting in a wheelchair at the time, and even though she was almost eighty, and even though she looked more like a reigning monarch than like Willie ("the Actor") Sutton.

Listening to her words, however, I could imagine it: M. F. K. Fisher, head held high, small smirk on her slightly pursed lips, walks by the Bank of America carrying her most formal black-sequined evening bag, sleek and thick as a brick. Then, as the bank guard at the doorway looks aside—those bank guards who exist only in movies and dreams—she daintily extracts the cement-encrusted battered old brick from its sequined bunting. Taking a quick and appropriately furtive look right and left, she winds up, makes the pitch, and—crash—the glass facade of the Bank of America cracks apart, allowing her to rush in and empty the vaults and tills and safes. She had, she admitted, only one hesitation. She would have to pull this heist outside the country, "because I wouldn't want to embarrass Rex."

Her father, Rex Kennedy, exerts strong taming influences. Though he died almost forty years ago, he continues to serve as mentor, judge, role model, and respected dispenser of praise and punishments. Or perhaps it is she, his daughter, who continues his roles, because she has to, or likes to, or for whatever reason. But he is always there, brought in for contrast, comparison, or comment at everything but bank robberies.

After revealing her larcenous proclivities that day in 1987, she announced that she had come to the Stanford Court to celebrate "more or less," her fiftieth anniversary: "Fifty years in publishing," she said, sounding a tone between pride and sarcasm. Rex had been there in 1937 when she published her first book, *Serve It Forth*, dedicated to her parents: "For R. B. K. & E. O. H. K." In fact, the three of these extravagantly initialed family members were sitting down at the dinner table in 1937 when Mary Frances asked if they had received a copy of her new book.

Vividly she reenacted their lack of enthusiasm, playing the part of both parents with the total recall of an incensed child:

"Oh, your book. I don't think we've seen anything."

"Have we received Dote's book?"

"I don't remember seeing any book."

"Book?"

Her face flickered with emotion, her eyes flashed iridescence, blues and grays; her cheeks reddened. It was not anger but the excitement of telling a captivating story.

"Well they just couldn't seem to remember. I was so upset. Finally I banged my hands on the table and said, 'Goddamn it. You treat me as if I had tertiary syphilis.' As I banged the table, the bottle of wine shook. Oh, Rex was furious."

Now she stopped to smile.

"Just furious. 'Doty,' he said, 'leave the table.' Here I was, thirty years old, actually walking away from the table."

She stomped out of the room, feeling half like a naughty child and half like a humiliated grown woman. Once she had closed the door behind her, the absurdity of the situation caught up with her. She started to laugh. Through the door she could hear them, Father and Mother, Rex and Edith. They were laughing, too.

"I came back in, and we all apologized to each other, but that's the way it was. The ability to write decently was just assumed in the family. I published five books before anyone at home even noticed," she explained. "But I remember the first time Rex made me leave the table for saying something that he considered obscene. I was, oh, fourteen."

"Do you remember the word?" I asked, sure that no

one ever forgets this high point in life, the unexpected escape of the first swearword in the presence of the horrified-speechless parents, the end of innocence, their innocence.

"Oh, yes," she said, one pinkie stuck elegantly into the air as she lifted her wine glass slowly, with regal grace. "Turd."

For a moment even I was caught off guard. It was, to put it mildly, not her sort of word. She looked so queenly this day, due in part to the majesty of the surroundings. She took them on, like a chameleon, using them for effect and for fun.

"That was nothing," she was explaining, "compared to this bastard business."

"Bastard?" Obviously she had decided that, in this impeccably proper setting, something a little scabrous would add just the right note: She proceeded blithely from *turd* to *bastard*.

"I was misquoted," she protested, before I even knew what she was referring to. "Nevertheless, everyone in Whittier was scandalized," she went on, smiling.

"In Whittier?" I was confused.

She explained that her childhood hometown had recently held its centennial and that she was invited as one of the town's eminent *émigrées*. This event struck me as the kind of affair she loves to be invited to so she can say no. But for some reason she accepted. Perhaps it was the fact that her fiftieth publishing anniversary coincided with the one hundredth anniversary of the small Quaker town in which she spent her childhood and about which she wrote *Among Friends*. Or maybe it was the promised accommodations, at the Whittier Hilton.

"The Whittier Hilton," she said, chuckling. "Can you imagine? They don't even realize how funny it is, the idea of a Hilton in Whittier. Rex would have died laughing." She laughed out loud, maybe the way he would have.

"It was a very modern hotel, you know. The very latest buttons to push, everything electronic. Nothing like this place." She waved her right hand up and down, to make sure I was getting her point. The Stanford Court was plush but classic, with no sense of electronics, though they were there, as they must be. The Whittier Hilton's electronics were more obvious, especially when they malfunctioned, leaving all the hotel guests, including Mary Frances and her traveling companion, locked in their rooms. Fortunately they had food, bowls of fruit mostly.

"Still, it was pretty awful," she said, "the feeling of being imprisoned. Like jail." She shuddered. "Rex would have died," she added. She had even less patience with the organizers of the Whittier Centennial. I was still waiting for her to tell about the "bastard business."

"They didn't even mention Rex, even though he ran *The Whittier News* for over forty years." He was also a member of the Whittier Rotary Club, president of the Whittier Chamber of Commerce, an exalted Ruler of the Elks, a member of the Free and Accepted Masons, a member of Al Malaikah Shrine, and a congregant of Saint Mathias Episcopal Church.

Although the centennial people managed to overlook all these achievements, they did honor Mary Frances, along with a "certain president" she characterized with the phrase "always was tricky." Though almost two generations had passed since Rex's death in 1953, his daughter thought it ironic and unfair that people knew her first and him second or, possibly, did not know him at all. In Dijon she was a wife; in Switzerland, a writer; in Saint Helena, a mother; but in Whittier she was, and always will be, a daughter. I smiled at her sideways, trying to pry back open a smile, trying to say that I know the feeling, that you can't get mad at people just because they acknowledge your fame, just because they think you're more important than your father. I tried to say this without getting too direct about the matter. I knew when I was trespassing close to the edge. I did not enter the Fatherland with psychological chips on my shoulder. I did not even mention, one time when I sat in her living room while she flitted about in her kitchen making lunch, the fact that she was whistling "Oh, My Papa." I am a friend. I am there for the ride, whatever rides we can go on together, and they are usually good ones. I do not talk about Oedipus and Rex in the same sentence, as if I'm so smart. I do not want my head, as my mother so often offered, handed to me, not even metaphorically.

"Tell me about the Whittier swearword," I said instead.

"Oh, yes, well," she came back quickly, clearing her throat. "Well, someone quoted me as saying that all Quakers were bastards. What I really said was that *some* Quakers are bastards, and *some* are very nice." She fussed a bit more about this inequity, pulling her black fringed shawl about her, muttering the name Cleveland Amory as the culprit responsible for the alleged misquote in his review of *Among Friends.*

Nevertheless, she is the first to admit that in her family it is an honored tradition to get in trouble because of one's ornery words. A fifth-generation writer with Scottish and Irish newspaper people loitering among her heritage, she follows a great-grandfather whose leaflets against Queen Victoria won him a death sentence (he got out, so she says, just in time) and a midwestern grandfather whose provocative editorials impelled him toward a peripatetic life style, to escape the wrath of the offended. Rex's newspaper career also had its pugilistic aspects, though through no fault of his own.

"Rex started out in Chicago as a goon for Colonel McCormick," she said, and I said, "A goon? For Colonel who?"

It seems that Rex went to work for Colonel McCormick at the "other" Chicago newspaper—"the one not owned by William Randolph Hearst," she explained—the *Chicago Tribune.*

"The delivery boys from the Hearst newspaper would beat up the boys who delivered Colonel McCormick's *Trib.* The Hearst forces outnumbered the colonel's boys three to one. Finally Colonel McCormick enlisted the services of two of his reporters, who also happened to be former football players from the University of Chicago—Rex and his brother Walt—to protect the *Trib*'s delivery boys.

"McCormick called them Stagg's men, after their coach's name, Amos Alonzo Stagg.

"Uncle Walt was built like a ton of bricks, broad shoulders," she described, pulling up her shoulders and upper arms to simulate her uncle's quarter ton of billowing hulk but looking more like a baby wren about to fly for the first time. "Whereas Rex," she laughed with an affectionate sigh, "well, he had the broad shoulders, all right, but he was thinner, much thinner; long bones, you know."

I tried to imagine him, remembering some pictures I'd seen.

"He was only on the team at the University of Chicago because he came in after Walt, who was the big star, but the coach wanted Rex on the team, too. Stagg was very powerful, 'the old man of football,' they called him."

Not only did the brothers manage to protect McCormick's newsboys from the Hearst "thugs," but they made a big impression on William Randolph himself.

"Hearst always hated Rex from then on. All through his career."

In true Kennedy fashion, her father and uncle did eventually leave town. They moved on to Albion, Michigan, where they bought and ran *The Albion Recorder*. It was the kind of town where the fire department hooked up its hoses and sprayed the Kennedy home to cool it down on the day Mary Frances was born, July 3, 1908.

"It was a sweltering hot day," Mary Frances re-counted with all the detail of a reporter assigned to cover the event instead of the infant being born. "It was Rex who got them to do it." About two years later Rex decided to leave this town also and to sever the four-generation thread of newspaperism. He sold his interest in the paper to his brother.

"He decided he wanted to become a geologist," Mary Frances announced in the resigned, airless voice that women use to describe the cataclysmic, tradition-shattering, crackpot schemes of the men they have had to contend with. "And so we went to Puget Sound."

"Oh, Washington?" I said, trying to imagine her in the wilds of the Pacific Northwest. "Did you like it there?"

"I was about two," she informed me, her eyes looking away from mine as if she was trying to think of something else. "I don't remember much of it."

"And did he really work as a geologist up there?"

"No, he was mostly a beachcomber. Mother, too. The whole thing was an attempt to escape the family destiny, journalism. They stayed there till the money ran out."

I was curious about how he was then able to buy the Whittier town paper.

"Grandmother Holbrook bought it for him," she ex-plained. "He ran it, of course."

He must have been more tactful about his opinions than his forebears, since the family was never run out of Whittier. They didn't have to be run out, judging from Mary Frances's descriptions of Quaker attitudes in Whittier; they could stay right where they were and be effectively excluded. Maybe that's what she meant by "bastards." At any rate, Rex's opinions and preferences within their household had lasting effects. Not only did they continue to this day, helping to prevent unruly daughters like Mary Frances from robbing banks, but they were responsible for her very name as a writer: M. F. K. Fisher.

"You see, I'd sold a story to *Westways* magazine for money," she explained, sounding guiltier than any mere bank robber. "I used the byline Fisher because I didn't want my father to know that I had taken money. I got ten dollars for the story, but I got twenty-five for the drawings."

"When was this?" I asked, imagining she must have been a young child but realizing that it had to have been after she married Al Fisher, or she wouldn't have had his name to pin on at the end.

"Oh, about 1934," she said. "I guess I was twenty-five, twenty-six," she added, getting my point.

"Of course, it was silly to think I could avoid my father, since he had helped found the damn thing." Some of his friends had started *Westways* as a kind of house organ for the Southern California Automobile Association.

"That started the whole damn silly business about M. F. K. Fisher," she said. Naturally many people—including, at first, Hamish Hamilton, the publisher of her first book—thought M. F. K. Fisher was a man. "He was astonished to meet me," she said with a self-satisfied smirk.

"So I was very 'ambisexual' from the word go, I guess," she said wistfully, enigmatically.

"Do you think things would have worked this way for someone named Mary Kennedy?" I asked with a teasing smile, trying to imagine her decked out in such tame and ordinary nomenclature as these, her maiden names.

"I tried to change it," she said, but once she was becoming known, it was futile. "But I am Mary Frances, not MFK," she asserted. "When people call me that, I know they don't know me at all."

I ask her about her mother's name; was she ever nicknamed EOHK?

"Edith Oliver Holbrook Kennedy," she pronounced, acknowledging that her mother's four-part name might have whetted her own interest in elongated strings of anonymous initials. But she never gives her mother much credit or dwells on Edith for very long. One exception was the story she told next, about how Edith "cornered the market" on the town librarians, getting them to order the books she thought should be available.

"And every Christmas she would give them nightgowns, big, white, expensive. They never saw anything like it. And when Mother died . . ."—she stopped to calculate—"thirty-five or forty years later, one of the librarians wrote me a letter telling me how wonderful those nightgowns were.

"Still, they never would order copies of Krafft-Ebing's *Psychopathia Sexualis* or Radclyffe Hall's *Well of Loneliness* or anything too lesbian, Freudian, or sexual. So she bought them herself."

"Your mother bought books for the library?" I asked.

"No, for our home." She answered curtly but with a provocative incompletion in her voice. I fell into this trap, as always. "And why did she want them?" I asked, unaware that I was about to discover something about the boarding school that Edith shipped her eldest daughter off to in her early teens.

"All the girls fell in love with me," she said flatly with a shrug. "And most of the teachers, too. I was attractive to them, for some reason."

When she came home and told her mother, Edith advised her to read a few of those books. But they didn't have them in the library, so Edith bought them herself.

"Wasn't she upset to discover that she had put you in that situation?" I asked, trying to imagine my own mother accepting with equanimity such a revelation about the bastion of chastity, Sacred Heart Academy, that I attended.

"Oh, no. She *knew.*" She said it like that, emphasis on *knew.* She went on to say that she had never really minded going to boarding school, which she attended with her younger sister Anne. It was better than being a mother to the two little ones, Norah and David, whom she felt she had charge of since the day they were born.

"I feel like I became a mother when I was nine years old. After Norah and David were born, Mother took to her bed."

I was not unaware, and neither was she, that statements like these have prompted analyses of her work that approach Freudian proportions. And though she protests that she never reads anything written about her, favorable or otherwise, somehow she manages to get all the details and innuendos of any reference to her. Furthermore, she always has ready a saber-sharp reply. One of these probes into her privately held psychology elicited the response: "I started to read it; I just howled," followed by her own précis of the author: "She's the one who should be analyzed . . . like most doctors." So I said nothing too presumptuous, even when she summed up with tempting, double-dare-you bait like "I loved my mother, and I—" And then she stopped and started over: "Well, I didn't love her, but I thought she was a fascinating woman."

Rex, on the other hand, seems to have been fascinating as well as loved; he was a force, a presence, from morning till night. Her body loosened up and her face relaxed when she returned to Rex and how he "always read three newspapers at the breakfast table." She described how he would sit down and perfunctorily ask how they all were.

"We would always say fine, fine." She recounted the scene: four child-sized heads bobbing around the table. Except that one morning her brother said he wasn't feeling well. This tremendous break in protocol was so upsetting her father put down the paper and addressed little David directly. From her nuances, not her words, I got the feeling Rex was more disturbed at the rift in routine than by her brother's health. At any rate, David dutifully reiterated his sick feelings, excused himself, and went back up to bed. At that point everything returned to normal. Balance was reestablished. All was right with the world, except possibly for David.

The next time they would see each other was at the dinner table. But the important things happened later, not at dinner but just after.

"Where shall we go tonight?" Rex would ask. Edith would leave the table to seclude herself in "her little apartment," as Mary Frances called it, just off the dining room. Then Mary Frances and Rex would go on their white-wine trips.

"Mother would always retire from these discussions. She called them arguments."

They seemed to be more like flights of fancy, imaginary excursions that they would plan around the world or to some specific island in the Caribbean. Their fantasized itineraries included the chartering of old freighters and leisurely travels down to the Panama Canal.

"Rex loved going to Mexico," Mary Frances sighed, a small catch in her voice. Eventually one of these white-wine trips turned into a reality.

"We kidnapped Rex once," she chuckled, her not-so-latent outlaw instincts surfacing once again. The whole family was in on it, plus a friend who was the captain of a Swedish freighter. Before Rex knew what was happening, he and Edith were out to sea, heading for the heretofore imaginary canal and, ultimately, Amsterdam and Switzerland.

"That was a white-wine trip that really took off," she

laughed, adding a bit sadly, "but they were all very real when they happened."

For a moment I felt as if I might soon be on a white-wine trip of my own as I finished the last crisp drop in my glass and watched her refilling it. The feeling was sufficiently fortifying to allow me to make an analogy that had been lurking. I told her about sitting around the after-dinner table in my family. I would try to engage my father in conversation, not only because it was interesting to talk to him about something—current events, mythology, science—but also because my mother, if I was involved with my father, would eventually decide she might as well do the dishes alone. Most of all, I enjoyed the role reversal: taking my mother's place as a companion at the dinner table, and having her take my place as the washer of the dishes. Mary Frances laughed and shook her head, as if recognizing the similarity of our experiences.

"Yes, I see what you mean," she said, "but that wasn't my situation. For one thing, Father had a rule that we never spoke at table about politics, sex, or religion. And also, Mother was present the whole time, even though she was in the next room."

She would go off to read her book. "She was always reading a book. You know, pretending to read. But she was listening the whole time. We could hear her chuckling in there once in awhile."

She never had the sense of monopolizing her father that I did.

"To tell the truth, I once wrote a poem about it," I

confessed, narrowing my eyes as I tried to squeeze the words out of my Chardonnayed brain. "Dad ate green grapes. Mom cleared the table, and I started avoiding the dishes by asking my father, 'How come . . .?'" But that was all I could remember, or wanted to.

"I'll send it to you some time," I offered, half in jest.

"I look forward to reading it, dear," she smiled.

I went back to concentrating on her wine trips. Were they prescient or causal, I wondered for a moment, remembering all the freighters and ships she did travel on as soon as she left home: her first ship, the *Berengaria*, which she took with her new husband, Al Fisher, to Dijon; then back to California on the Cunard line; later the Italian freighter *Feltre*; a Dutch passenger freighter; the *Ile de France*, the *De Grasse*; the *Normandie*—all within a decade or so. Her white-wine trips were like programming; her life, wish fulfillment.

Did she choose to leave the country to live her life for the same reason she would choose to leave the country to rob a bank: so she wouldn't embarrass Rex? Or maybe she had to be truly out of his reach in order to flourish on her own? While I teetered dangerously on these foggy psychoanalytical precipices, Mary Frances began to describe another of Rex's domains: the spanking department.

When he came home from work, her mother would indicate which of the children required paddling, and he would execute the deed. With the girls—and there were three out of four—the paddling stopped, for modesty's sake, at a fairly young age.

"Thus allowing criminal tendencies to flourish unchecked in those of the girls so inclined," I added with a kind of Sherlock Holmes coups de grace.

That was only one of the good things about being a girl of a certain age, it turned out. Shortly afterward Mary Frances went off to boarding school and decided to write her father a letter. In it she asked a question she hadn't dared ask in person: could she call him Rex?

"He wrote back and said all his friends call him Rex. And I was his friend. So, yes, why shouldn't I call him Rex?"

She reported this with a look of total satisfaction, bashful and proud. She has been calling him Rex ever since, every chance she gets.

Popcorn
Oxtail Stew

"SHUT UP AND EAT YOUR POPCORN."

The words flew by me, or vice versa, as I huffed and puffed back into her house.

Popcorn was a word I hadn't expected to encounter in M. F. K. Fisher's house. In fact, I dreaded those discussions of what you eat when you're alone, because I would have had to confess a bunch of things that were not in my image of her image of me.

Yes, I made popcorn, and yes, I put salt on it, and yes, I brought it into my bedroom, and yes—oh, no, not this, I could never admit this—I turned on the VCR, shoved in some old *film noir* or *Thin Man,* and ate the whole salted bowlful. She has written with such dignity of eating alone: the silent ceremonies of setting a place, filling the crystal wine glass, time reserved and respected, like a sacrament that you could actually enjoy. You could be a guest in your own soul, honored, paid attention to, nourished, and edified. I knew she'd written something like that, felt that way. It didn't sound like she was talking about chomping down a big bowl of popcorn.

But there it was: "SHUT UP AND EAT YOUR POPCORN" tacked to the bulletin board at the entranceway.

This entranceway was a little different lately; in fact, everything had changed a bit since Mary Frances had had the spacious outside porch walled up and turned into a bedroom for Mary Jane, her first live-in helper. Mary Jane had been spending most of the day there anyway, doing errands, taking care of the driving, generally helping out. But the new room meant that the porch's work—drying herbs, storing boxes of blood oranges and crates of melons, sequestering champagne, caring for these endless food-gifts people gathered for Mary Frances from their own yards and gardens, orchards and vineyards—had to be done inside now. It crowded things up around the kitchen sink and filled the couches and windowsills, covered the corner desk and the dining-room table, affected the balance in many ways.

But the room was there now, permanently, and Mary Jane was there for however long Mary Frances felt she needed her services. Nor was Mary Jane unobtrusive. Her presence was palpable, had visible consequences. On my last visit I even noticed a television in the living room, incongruous in its setting near the wood-burning iron fireplace. Mary Frances made it quite clear that it was not really a television since it did not receive signals or show "TV programs," or do things like that, all of which sounded vaguely immoral the way she described them. This one just played movies and tapes, and besides, the whole thing was Mary Jane's idea: "I have no interest in it whatever."

I paused at the bulletin board long enough to note that an article about shutting up and eating your popcorn had been clipped from a July 1986 issue of the *San Francisco Chronicle*. Why? I wondered.

"Oh, you're back from your walk," called a bright, surprised voice coming toward me from the living room. Mary Frances was smiling up from the bottom of the three steps, where she was sitting in her wheelchair. As I walked down the steps, she pushed the chair away and strode over to the couch. If I thought for one minute she needed that wheelchair, she showed me otherwise.

"You didn't see any snakes, I guess."

She rolled her eyes to the side so I couldn't tell whether she was kidding about the snakes or feeling guilty that she hadn't mentioned them before.

"Where did you go, dear?" she asked, finding one long stray hair to tuck with the rest, neat and wavy, like corn tassles. She anchored it somewhere behind her neck.

"I walked all over Bouverie Ranch. Nearly broke my neck on the cow grate, or whatever you call those iron bars that are planted across the walkway. Or are they to keep out the snakes?" I asked, not wanting to know. I was wondering whether there wasn't some truth to the sign at the gate stating that "TRESPASSERS WILL BE VIOLATED." "Then I walked down Dunbar Road past the Arabian-horse farm and in front of Waterman's Bread and Breakfast, where Joan is staying, I understand."

Joan was the woman whom I had met there that morning. She was thumbing through cookbooks and various editions of Mary Frances's books, jotting down publication dates. She was working on a book about Mary Frances, Julia Child, and Alice Waters, Joan explained to me, about what she calls their cuisine personae. That was just one of the things going on at Mary Frances's that day. I never could figure out how she kept them straight, not to mention participated in most of them.

"But are you going someplace?" I asked, noting her newly applied bright lipstick, the soft blue eye shadow, and pinked cheeks. She was wearing a pair of Adidas and a purple velour jogging-style outfit. She looked rosy from its reflection, as if she could sprint out at any minute.

I didn't want her to say yes. I was looking forward to spending the time with her. Lately it seemed there was never any time, quiet uninterrupted, chatting-it-up time. Someone was always around.

"No, I'm staying right here," she said reassuringly, adding that she had set aside the afternoon—"after you've come all this way"—so we could go over some things. But first, she warned me, she was expecting a visit from her nephew, John Barr, and his teenage son, Oliver, who were visiting Norah in Jenner. They live in Boston, and Mary Frances hadn't seen them in seven years. John does something ultrasecret, she started to tell me, but the next minute they were there: handsome as oak trees, crisp as an October breeze on the Charles River, efficient as easterners. I thought John had that watchful dignity of those who have packed away something secret behind their eyeballs and don't want you to see in; but probably I was just imagining it. As I looked at him, though, I couldn't help remembering Mary Frances's story about him as a child of seven or eight. One day at the ranch he was "picking on" her daughter Kennedy. When Mary Frances reprimanded him, he asked her insolently, "Who do you think you are? The boss of the whole world?"

I left to take another walk, my mind a tangle of potential snakes. It never seemed to end, this lovely rolling acreage of the Bouverie Ranch, owned by the architect David Bouverie, who lived in the big house behind the vineyard. A long-time admirer of Mary Frances and her work, Bouverie had often visited her in her five-bedroom Victorian at 1467 Oak Street in Saint Helena. He tried to convince her that with her daughters gone the big house would be too much for her, and he offered to design her a hideaway on his five-hundred-acre estate in Glen Ellen. He tried to emphasize the air of respectability that she would lend the place, but they both laughed at the inevitable tittering and gossip that they knew would accompany her tenancy. Eventually they worked out a gentleman's agreement—"It took seven lawyers to draw it up," she once told me—and in 1970 she sold her house, turned the money over to Bouverie, and went to France. While she was gone, he built her this personal-sized California-wine-country hacienda, a place from which you can smell the grapes growing. It was just what she'd wanted at the time.

In fact, she had laid out her plans for its construction,

not in blueprints but in no uncertain terms. She knew not only that she was an incurable bibliophile but how that passion should be translated into a physical structure. She called her finished house, a two-room bungalow of curved wooden ceilings and rounded doorways and generous balconies, her *palazzina*. But what it really is, underneath it all, is one enormous bookcase.

Every room is a succession of shelves bulging with books; and although she may have reserved some closets for the more traditional function of storing clothes and shoes, most of them are stacked with copies of books, hers or other peoples'. As for walls, there are a few here and there, used to connect the bookcases, hold the house up, and display the bright paintings and artwork she wants to be surrounded by.

Black-tiled floors lead everywhere, ending at the doorway of the sanctum sanctorum. This is the bathroom, with a tub you could camp out in, a room-sized shower, and lipstick-red walls lined with paintings. The tiles here are a gold-flecked gray, the color of fox fur; the sinks, marble. It is more of a mood piece than a bathroom.

Nothing about the house—which she often referred to as Last House—had changed since the day she moved in, until now. The added room was a distortion of the original plan, in more ways than one. From now on someone besides Mary Frances would be staying on the premises.

Even though she was isolated, up here in the hills, she had no interest in proximate companionship. Her independent nature writhed against the idea. It was no longer a matter of choice, however. She had been suffering from Parkinson's disease for several years, and in addition her hip-replacement operations had not been completely successful. She had recently written a note to herself: "This was the Lost Summer, indeed! A new eye, a new hip, and on Sunday, in the first gentle rain of autumn, I hobble happily into the last days of October." But she often found it easier physically, though not psychologically, to resort to a wheelchair.

She was no longer able to ramble around the grass-quilted hills and slopes, which took more agility than I had suspected, as I noticed during my second walk of the day. In this rural, winery-dotted countryside, people drove their cars like ammunition. Before I reached the top of the first grapevine-covered hill, I could see John Barr's car pulling out of the driveway; maybe he was afraid that if he stayed around too long, he'd start to get bossed around again. When I got back to the house, I noticed the sign on the door, another addition necessitated by the new room. It was just a piece of white note paper on which Mary Frances had scribbled "Friends: Ring bell and come in. Foes: Enter (any old way)."

In the living room I found Mary Frances reading a pile of papers, the mail perhaps. Through her makeup she looked pale or shaken or disappointed or all three. Before I could figure out what to say, I heard the question: "How about some of that Bombay gin?"

Bombay gin? It sounded so purposeful, a real drink,

not like the crisp white wines or local mountain ales Mary Frances usually offered. Bombay gin sounded more like Fisherman's Wharf or San Diego or Minneapolis than Sonoma. It didn't sound like her. It wasn't her; it was Mary Jane.

Mary Frances was in fact climbing the three steps up into the hallway that led to her room. One hand was already waving no before she said, "No. You two go ahead. I'll join you in a bit."

Mary Jane was standing near the glass door, sliding it open so we could sit out on the front patio. She was one of the few people I'd ever met who was shorter than I, about five foot one-half inch. She wore denim, jeans and top, and serious-looking Reeboks. She was pouring Bombay gin into two squat, ice-filled glasses.

"This is special," she was saying. "I don't share this with just anybody."

"Do you have any tonic?" I asked.

Her pouring arm froze in midair. She looked at me. In her tanned, impish face, her eyes had suddenly turned suspicious.

"If you want to mix it, we have some other stuff. I mean, you wouldn't want to adulterate the Bombay gin, I mean . . . there's some Gilbey's here. . . ."

Her voice trailed off. What had I done? *Adulterate.* Sounded worse that adultery. Quickly I rescinded my insensitive request and walked out onto the patio with her and our two hefty, neat gins. The parched, wheat colored grass lay everywhere, in every direction; its honey browns and dull golds might drift on forever, but for the sharp black line of Sonoma Highway in the distance.

I found myself reciting some lines about "the world which lies before us like a land of dreams, so glorious, so beautiful, so new. . . ." and then stopping suddenly. "Just a remnant of some long-ago English lit class," I told Mary Jane, embarrassed by this uncontrollable effusion. It was such a generous incipient afternoon; something had to be said, irrelevant though it may be. More to the point, even geographically, was what Mary Frances had written when she invited me up for these few days. "Come in October," she had scribbled in the margin, "the air like wine."

Suddenly I noticed four brilliant flowers, purple-blue, almost iridescent, their glistening green stems growing— they couldn't be growing—among the gentle tufts of lifeless hay on the other side of the balcony just below us.

Mary Jane laughed and said that they often throw "used" flowers "and other things" over the side "for our little friends, who usually take them away. They used to throw more things over—melons and things—but one day David Bouverie was showing some people around the ranch just as Mary Frances pitched out a cantaloupe. He came over later and said, "Mrs. Fisher, this is not a dispose-all." So they've cut down a bit, "but we still do it," she admitted, chuckling like a cartoon chipmunk.

I liked talking to Mary Jane in a way. But it was like getting the other side of the picture when I didn't want the other side of the picture. I wanted to talk to Mary Frances;

that's what I was there for. As if on cue, Mary Frances came swirling into the room, reminding me of "The Loretta Young Show." She even looked a bit like her at that moment, with that big audience-pleasing smile which should have been vacuous but wasn't.

"Shall I make your drink, Mary Frances?" asked Mary Jane. Her drink, as I knew by then, was Campari, gin, and vermouth in a proportion that makes the result a neon orange. I think it was the color she wanted; she never seemed to drink the stuff.

"Yes, please, Mary Jane. But plain old Gilbey's is good enough for me."

She said this as if we were the elitists in town, we with our Bombay bombast, our preferences. Mary Frances, by contrast, emerged as the person of simple tastes, the purist. She was down-to-earth, plain spoken, unpretentious, while we were the fussy old biddies. The look on Mary Jane's face summed up our position: we walked right into that one.

"Tell me when you want to eat," Mary Frances ordered invitingly as we finished our supergins. She explained that they had been eating at odd hours recently because of the VCR. They had accumulated a small library of movies, a dozen or so, and every time they watched one, Mary Frances recounted with more than a scintilla of annoyance, they ended up having dinner late.

"We spend hours eating popcorn," Mary Frances complained, "and by the time we're supposed to have dinner, I have no appetite left."

"You have to put lots of butter on it," said Mary Jane,

oblivious to, or ignoring this quibble, "and then the secret ingredient, a dash of that yeast."

"We get the yeast at the health-food store," added Mary Frances. "It's the only place that has it."

As for the popcorn, continued Mary Jane, "we find that Blue Eyes' popcorn—you know, Paul Newman's—is better than old Rechenbacher, or whatever his name is."

"You just like looking at his face on the box," I ventured, "although I wouldn't know; I just buy the generic." This should make up for the Bombay gin, I found myself thinking victoriously.

"There's an article on the bulletin board that relates to all this," Mary Jane announced. "It's called 'SHUT UP AND EAT YOUR POPCORN.' "

"Yes, I noticed. I was wondering what it could possibly have to do with you two. Now I know."

I was surprised at the enthusiasm with which Mary Frances spoke about utilizing the VCR, that ignoble electronic TV mechanism she so disdained previously. The admission was made, somewhere in there, that the fixture had been transmogrified from something that just played tapes into a real television set. Not only that, but Mary Frances admitted to actively looking forward to watching two Japanese horror films someone had just lent them. Of course, she knows quite a bit about the film world, I thought, having worked in Hollywood. Probably a professional interest.

Suddenly we heard music coming from somewhere, as if the whole room had burst into song. I looked around, puzzled, but Mary Frances was not in the least concerned. Just as suddenly the music stopped. Then I noticed that she was holding some remote-control device. She handed it to me explaining, "Any time I want to hear the latest news, I switch on the radio with this. It's quite handy. The only problem is if I drop a plate on the floor or something, the radio goes on also."

With that she reached for a bread board and let it fall. The music immediately came marching back. Unfortunately the bread board split in two.

"Oh well," she sighed. "That's what I get for showing off."

"I never thought I'd have to come to Glen Ellen to witness the latest technology," I said, fitting the two pieces of wood together. "Maybe I can fix this."

"Forget about it," she said, already busy with something else at the stove. She started to tell me about children with arthritis and how terrible it is.

"I've been trying to work out some recipes the children can do with their poor crippled little fingers. These are some chocolate drop cookies," she said, removing a tray of round blobs from the oven. "They'll be able to make these all right."

I noticed, as she tested the firmness of the cookies, how twisted her own hands had become from arthritis. She was mumbling about something, but the only word I heard distinctly was *Crusties.*

"And did you ever have Crusties?" Mary Jane asked me. Never knowingly, I admitted, unless someone had slipped me one anonymously, someone like my little daughter, from the sound of it. Mary Jane then revealed, to my astonishment, that Mary Frances was interested in Crusties, which she'd heard advertised on the radio. They come in two types: the French crepe type and the fluffy pancake type, and they are ready-made; all you do is pop them in the toaster.

"Might as well try them," said Mary Frances with more resignation than enthusiasm, I thought. It was becoming obvious that Mary Jane was not, by talent or inclination, a cook, and that Mary Frances had little time and energy these days for culinary endeavors.

Mary Jane mentioned something about a program they had seen about Gertrude Stein and Alice B. Toklas, which she liked very much but Mary Frances thought awful. It was funny but also sad to see them argue, especially when Mary Jane said something like, "Nobody made you stay in the room to watch it," and Mary Frances said that Mary Jane identified with "the little dwarf" who played the part of Toklas.

Then they both laughed, but it didn't clear away the residue—resentment, was it? Mary Jane had introduced a new element into life at the Bouverie Ranch. The VCR and its aftermath—popcorn, Crusties—were things they could share, have in common. Maybe it wasn't such a great idea.

But then Mary Frances said she would soon have to learn to operate the VCR herself, because Mary Jane was going away for a reunion or something. I thought it was temporary, but it turned out to be otherwise. At Mary

Frances's request Mary Jane never returned. To Mary Frances her own independence was more important than the mobility and general all-around assistance that Mary Jane had, in her relatively short tenure, so amply provided.

"I might want to watch 'M*A*S*H*' or something," Mary Frances said with that snake look, half-kidding, half-guilty. I decided to change the subject.

"Did you ever see an early-forties movie called *Quiet Please, Murder?* I think they named it that because it takes place in a library. Anyway, some time during the movie a woman comes wandering into the reference room saying something like, 'I want that book about the wolf, about cooking a wolf. I think it's called *How to Cook a Wolf.*' I was so surprised. Have you ever seen it, Mary Frances? It stars George Sanders, Richard Denning, and the director is John Larkin."

Mary Frances laughed. She said she didn't know that movie, but she had heard that *How to Cook a Wolf* was filed in the Library of Congress under biology.

She decided it was time to put dinner together, a process that had been going on all along, though we were unaware of it: the Japanese eggplants roasting in the oven, the mélange of prosciutto and potatoes and snow peas, one red tomato sliced thick and glistening.

Is this the moment to tell her about popcorn oxtail stew, I wondered. No, it isn't, I assured myself. There will never be the right moment for blundering into this one. But do it anyway. It kind of fits the mood.

"I may have just the answer for the late-meal VCR

dilemma. It came out of the research on fresh coriander I am doing for my herb and spice book. I discovered in a book about Pueblo and Navaho cooking a recipe for popcorn oxtail stew."

Mary Frances looked at me disbelieving. Pulling her lips back tight against her teeth, she made what my mother used to call "such a face." It was a "yuk" face, the envy of any modern-day, seven-year-old.

"Must be crunchy," she managed through clenched teeth, assuming that the corn kernels were to be used in their unpopped state. I explained that the recipe began with popping the corn and setting it aside.

"Then you cook the stew," I explained, "and just before serving, you ladle it into large bowls and sprinkle on the popped popcorn. So now you can have dinner and popcorn at the same time."

She mumbled something about how it might make a certain amount of sense, considering the alternative. But she didn't ask me to send the recipe.

We ate our meal with some icy cold gray Riesling and watched the blood-orange sun bed down behind the purple mountains. After Mary Jane went to her room, Mary Frances pointed out beyond the porch and started to giggle.

"Sometimes," she began in a tone both calculating and unrepentent, "we scatter flowers and things over the patio railing. Almost everything is carried off by the little mice and ants. Everything but orange peels and lemon peels—no one likes them."

The other reject, she discovered, was whole melons.

One day she threw out a little cantaloupe, and instead of breaking into pieces like she thought it would, it simply went "bounce bounce bounce across the field. Didn't break apart at all. David Bouverie happened to be walking through with someone just at that moment, and the other man kicked it with his foot. David told him, 'Oh, that's just Mary Frances. She uses this as her garbage dump.' "

I was about to tell her that Mary Jane had told me that same story a few hours earlier. But I suspected she might not like the idea of someone else telling her stories; she might consider it a challenge to her privacy. So I just said, "Nice garbage dump you have here, Mary Frances."

"Yes," she said, breathing in a mouthful of the dusk-cooled air. "I rather like it."

Birthday
Stories

M. F. K. Fisher was born on July 3, a date that particularly amuses her because, for one thing, it leads directly to one of her favorite stories.

"If I'd been born after midnight," she begins ominously, "they were going to call me Independencia." Her whole face glows with a fresh dose of relief at her narrow escape.

"And so I was born on the third." She announces this achievement with undisguised self-satisfaction, as if she had showed them.

"You know I start celebrating my birthday on the first of July and go right on through to Bastille Day, the fourteenth."

She never explains exactly why Bastille Day, but the identity with France is so obvious it seems unnecessary to ask. "I'd been waiting to go there all my life," she says of her first visit to France when she was twenty-one, "although I didn't know it until I got there." She seldom mentions that Bastille Day was also the birthday of her maternal grandmother, Mary Frances Oliver. This link with her namesake, born in 1839 in Dungannon, then in County Tyrone in northern Ireland, lends legitimacy to her claim to the date but adds nothing at all to the French connection. Or maybe Bastille Day is another independence day to add to her fortnight of nonstop personal celebrations. She likes celebrations, not flashy extravaganzas, but personal productions carried out with subtle yet palpable flourish, something into which a chilled bottle of Veuve Clicquot fits nicely. And birthdays—almost anybody's—give her a good excuse to tell one of her multitudinous birthday stories.

"I remember Rex's seventy-fifth birthday," she says. "We'd decided as a joke to serve him seventy-five chicken legs." She can't help laughing, just thinking about it: her distinguished newspaperman father sitting at the table before an important-looking platter filled to overflowing with seventy-five chicken legs.

"Actually," she admits, "he didn't think it was very funny. You know, old people don't always have such a good sense of humor about these things."

I wonder whether she thinks of herself as older now, as she tells this story, than her father was then. I wonder whether anybody would.

Another of her favorite birthday stories concerns her first husband, Al Fisher. One time he visited a gypsy, who told him that he would either be rich and famous or dead by the time he was thirty. So he approached his thirtieth year with the confidence that he would have arrived—somewhere—when the moment struck. But at the appointed hour there he was, alive and still pretty well unknown.

"He was furious," Mary Frances said with a mischievous chuckle, "just furious."

She was quite furious herself when, a few years ago on her birthday, her stove broke. She had invited me and another friend to her home to celebrate all of our summer birthdays at once. We both brought desserts. Mary Frances had planned to make some luncheon treats, but she hadn't got past the batch of hazelnut crescent cookies when bad stove things started happening.

The stove man arrived at almost the same moment as we did, but unlike us he was not given the opportunity to have a little Campari and white wine. Mary Frances led him directly to the offending equipment; at this point the afternoon's menu depended more on him than it did on her. I don't think she liked that idea one bit.

He must have felt our six eyes fixed firmly on his back, because every time he turned around, those same eyes attacked his chest. These were not the polite, coquettish glances of shy-away women; these were visual kicks in the pants, table-banging glares from three children waiting for their birthday party to begin.

Eventually it did begin, or rather it continued, complete with hot soup and fry-pan bread and hot coffee and three desserts—because, as Dylan Thomas said to excuse his Auntie Hannah's annual rum-tippling, "it was only once a year."

A few years ago Mary Frances and I exchanged birthday gifts near the end of June. It was closer to my birthday than to hers, but I don't think she minded, because it gave her a reason to extend her holidays even further, this time back a few days. She gave me a small wooden chest full of coated almonds and a bottle of wine vinegar made from fresh *herbes de Provence* steeped in good French white wine. I gave her a set of sixty petits fours tins in five different patterns.

When she opened the box, she was unable to hide her strong feelings: "Oh dear," she almost cried, "more things to make." But then she smiled quickly and reassured me that the tins would be fun to use and that soon she would send along the results. A year later, however, when I opened her birthday gift to me, there were the tins again, never used, untouched. I don't think she knew. But maybe she did.

The best thing about receiving a gift from Mary Frances is the background note that usually accompanies it. "It's from Provence," she informed me once as I opened a box in which lay a strange little pin with two figures, a man and a woman, dangling from a bar.

"*Santons* they're called, because originally they were statues of saints. They're part of the Christmas celebration in Marseille called *foire aux santons.* You can't imagine how many *santonniers* are out at their booths selling their tiny Marys and Jesuses and cradles and such. When they get tired of making the main characters, they start creating some of the bit players. These two are probably the mayor of Marseille and his wife."

She had several stories to tell about the lorgnettes she once offered me. We were sitting in my living room having a glass of wine before lunch when she pulled out a pair of fancifully decorated long-handled opera glasses. I thought they were magnificently archaic, like a parasol or a bustle or even a powdered wig.

"My daughters used to hate it when I would take these out in a restaurant in Provence to read the menu. They would just die. 'Mother, do you have to?' they would ask, mortified."

"They're beautiful, aren't they?" I said.

"Well I think so," she laughed. "Here," she said, handing them to me. "You keep them."

"Oh, I couldn't think of taking them," I responded. "I mean, you use them, don't you?" I was also thinking of her daughters; maybe she should give them to Kennedy or Anne, even if they had hated them once. Besides, as much as I wanted them, I didn't want the responsibility. They were part of her story, to hang onto and to tell. If I took them, they would soon become weighted down with new stories, and eventually some of the new stories wouldn't include her.

"Maybe for some other birthday," I suggested, watching regretfully as she put them away.

* * *

Her eightieth birthday began to be a problem over a year before it happened. Many of her friends wanted to "do something important" for this banner year, but no one knew just what. A few people got the idea of gathering quotations or greetings from everybody who knew her. One person wanted to publish the collection as a sort of festschrift. Another intended to present the tidy bundle of birthday letters as a gift. But everyone was afraid that whatever they were doing, no matter how pure their intentions, they would offend her. She did have these unpleasable tendencies: she hated it when people made a fuss, but she was insulted if they didn't. As her birthday grew closer and the pressure mounted, most people decided it was better to do the wrong thing, which was inevitable anyway, than to do nothing.

One of the most lavish of the wrong things was a dinner party given by a restaurant, whose owner invited a whole dining-room-ful of her "closest friends." On the night of the event, it was obvious that the guest list was well populated with members of the press and that the restaurant lost no opportunity to link its name with that of M. F. K. Fisher. If there was any subtlety to their approach, it went unnoticed by Mary Frances, who said after it was over, "I have never felt so used in my life."

One of the enigmas about this uncannily shrewd woman is that she does allow herself to be taken advantage of by the oddest assortment of people. Nevertheless, by the fourteenth of July 1988 the number of greetings and gifts that overcrowded her front hallway was almost more than she could cope with. The only way she could was by mass-producing the following letter:

> July 19, 1988
> Dear Friends:
>   This printed notice is shocking to me, but I know that you will understand and forgive it.
>   It brings you much more than my thanks, for all that you've done to make me a very happy person. Whether or not I am 80 years old, I know more than ever, because of everything you've sent me and done for me, that I am truly blessed among women.
>   Until I write decently to you, here then are all my thanks.

Her most fascinating birthday story is one she may be telling from now on. I heard it for the first time one summer day when we were sitting on her porch under the postcard-blue sky of the Sonoma wine country. From her high-backed wicker chair she pointed to the parched, flaxen field that stretches like an endless tatami mat all the way to the black-green mountains in the distance.

For sixteen years, she explained, on the day of her birthday or very close to it, a huge barn owl had flown across that field and landed on the telephone pole a few hundred yards from the porch. "It was at least three feet high, and it must have had a nine-foot wing span," she insisted, and it was definitely the same old owl year after year. But prior to her last birthday some people had come over with a sad story.

"They said they were sorry, but they'd found the owl, or rather the skeleton of the owl, on the grounds. A coyote had got him, they thought."

Sometime near her birthday, however, she was sitting on the same porch, in the same chair, looking out across the yellow-white hay. Suddenly a much smaller owl—"Maybe the grandson," she ventured—suddenly alighted on the aforementioned pole.

"Couldn't believe it," she said, both amused and bemused. She pulled her head back as if reality had some rightful place in her reveries, and then she said, "Well I don't expect it to happen again."

The Woman
Who Saved the
Gare de Lyon

I did not go to Paris to play M. F. K. Fisher, exactly.

But then one day on the Champs Élysées I saw the Café George V. It was a little place that unfolded out onto the sidewalk like one of those multitiered birthday cards with tables popping up on several different levels and tree branches jutting out sideways and lots of details painted in way in the background. Almost falling off the card on the right was a wrought-iron stand holding a menu almost totally obscured by the leaves of a potted tree. I sat down at the tiny table right in front of it, not because of its arboreal splendor but because it was the one farthest out on the sidewalk. I wanted to be able to see all the people walking by, hear their words and laughter and whatever songs they might be humming. But I wanted to be part of the restaurant as well, and the life that was going on behind me.

As soon as I sat down, I envisioned Greta Garbo as the Russian Ninotchka, newly arrived in Paris and instructing the French waiter in no-nonsense terms to bring her "raw beets and carrots."

"This is a restaurant, madam," responds the waiter almost tearfully, "not a meadow."

Somewhere among all these poses and delusions and exhilarating derangements I started feeling like playing not Greta Garbo but M. F. K. Fisher. She'd lived in Paris at one time, not far from here, in fact. She'd written of Paris, imbibed it, swallowed it, translated it, been changed forever by it. And something important here had possibly been changed forever by her in a way, something as important as the Gare de Lyon. Or, more precisely, it had *not* been changed because of her, if I had got the story right.

But as so often happened with Mary Frances and her elaborate stories, I never quite got it straight. I blame this phenomenon entirely on her, of course. It's because of her kaleidoscopic vision and her gift of total recall. She talks about something, gives the whole, full, richly detailed account: names, relationships, how surly they all were, why they were usually so boring, final fates of the principals involved. A few months later, if I refer to the story, picking up some detail to explore further, it never fails that I've got it all wrong.

"No, I never said that. Or at least I never meant it that way if it sounded like that."

And then she reenters the tale, turning the kaleidoscope a squeak so the same colored stones shift positions ever so slightly, but the picture changes completely. I hear the story again with the light glancing off different crystals. It is her story: that is the point. She doesn't like to be captured, caught in a moment, in a pose. People say, "Why don't you take a tape recorder with you so you can get everything down permanently and then you would have it?" I can think of nothing more ridiculous. When I am with her, we are laughing, we are wondering, we are twirling around. We have a relationship, not a recording session.

Still, with all this, I wanted to find out more about the incident between her and the Gare de Lyon. The last time I asked, I found myself hearing about her lifelong friendship with someone named Lawrence Powell.

"He's at the University of Arizona. He's emeritus now. But I've known him since Al Fisher and I lived in Dijon, almost fifty years ago. He was getting his doctorate at the University of Dijon, like Al."

"Did you used to go to the Gare de Lyon together, or something?" I asked, trying to veer back on course. But it was I who was off course.

"He wrote a book called *The Blue Train*," she continued, explaining that le Train Bleu was the name of the train that passed through the Gare de Lyon and also the name of the restaurant that sprawled regally along its second floor. "It's a very nice book, *The Blue Train*, a story of five love affairs, or maybe five stories," she corrected with a hint of sarcasm, "one love affair each."

"Oh," I said, my eyes widening. Love affairs. Fifty years. Now what? How do I ask the next question? I don't.

"And I saw him through all of those affairs, well four out of the five, anyway. He wrote the book in 1941, but he didn't publish it until 1977. The stories are all from the thirties, an American student in France; a little macho, you know, but nicely done."

The next thing I knew, I was, under her specific directions, crawling on the floor by the bookcase trying to read the titles of books that had been stacked there long enough to get dusty enough so I couldn't read the titles.

"It's there somewhere," she instructed me as I sneezed and sniffed my way through the overburdened shelves. I found quite a bit of Lawrence Clark Powell: *Robinson Jeffers: The Man and His Work* ("No, that's not it; that was his doctoral dissertation. He was writing that in Dijon when Al and I met him"); *Southwest Classics* ("No, that's not it; that's his specialty, really, the Southwest; his family background"); *A Passion for Books* ("No; he was/is quite a bookman, you know; spent years at UCLA before retiring and going to Arizona").

What am I doing this for? I wondered, as one fingernail hooked into the binding of a little book with an azure cover, dislodging it with more force than I had deemed necessary. I was persisting only because I hoped that if I ever found the damned thing it might help solve my self-created mystery of the *gare*.

"Ah, *The Blue Train*," I announced, holding it up in front of me so she could see it and I could see that I had indeed sacrificed one fingernail to the discovery process.

"This is a wonderful painting of the Gare de Lyon on the cover. Monet, isn't it?" I said—my little way of getting back on the subject of the Gare de Lyon.

"Yes, it is Monet," she said, reaching out with eager curving fingers for the book, "but it's the Gare Saint Lazare."

The next thing I knew we were listening to Henry Miller speaking about Paris. Mary Frances had several taped interviews in which he talked about the prostitutes and sipping cognac in the bistros and how the French have a dynamism that is different from you and me and how he would gladly give up art altogether if he thought it would feed one hungry person.

"I think he was getting carried away with himself there," Mary Frances said softly but reprovingly. "They admired each other very much," she went on. "Powell and Miller. In fact, he wrote the afterword for *The Blue Train*. They knew each other in Paris also. I must send him a copy of this tape, now that I think of it."

Listening to Henry Miller that day, I felt a glow of anticipation, knowing that I, too, would be in Paris in a few weeks. So on this night as I burrowed in behind my round table at Café George V, I was especially glad to be alone. I took out a notebook and started scribbling things down, the way she did, the way I imagined she did, anyway. She hadn't been in France since 1978. I wondered how she'd feel about all these flags plastered everywhere to celebrate the bicentennial or the merry-go-round in the Tuileries gardens flanked by tall, thin billboards announcing, "1989 LA RÉVOLUTION EST AUX TUILERIES." These signs further promised, both in French and dictionary English, "ALL ALONG THE FEAST, COMEDIANS AND MUSICIANS WILL COME FOR THE ENTERTAINMENTS OF THE PARK."

When the waiter came over, I did not order *café noir*, though I would have liked to, because I knew she didn't drink coffee. Nor did I order raw beets and carrots, because I was afraid, considering the way the world was heading, that they would have it. So I ordered red wine and sipped it for hours while the Egyptian hieroglyphs carved into the Concorde obelisk dissolved slowly into the smudged purple sky and my pen eventually ran out of ink.

I don't know if I felt like M. F. K. Fisher alone there in the café, "as if I were a fish in a bowl, watching another world through curved glass," as she once put it. But I felt very good (the *vin rouge, peut-être*). And once I even laughed out loud remembering her story of living on an expense account in Paris.

"I'd never had an expense account in my life," she recounted, still apparently breathless from this experience, which had happened almost a quarter century ago. She was there on assignment for Time-Life, writing the text for a book on the cooking of Provence.

"I asked them, "What do I do? How do I keep an expense account?' They said, 'Oh, just write everything down.' So I did. When I handed it in, they all howled, you know. I had two francs for this and five francs for that. They thought it was hilarious."

"What did you buy for two francs, anyway?" I asked, genuinely curious.

"Oh, I would buy the newspaper in Paris," she replied with a shrug. "Something like that."

"You were living in Paris but writing about Provence?"

"Yes. I had to go down quite often. So I would take the train. They all thought I was crazy. I should fly like anyone in their right mind. 'A waste of time,' they all pooh-poohed. But for me it was a kind of renewal, starting out at the Gare de Lyon."

"You mean the restaurant?" I asked, remembering her description of the Parma ham she once had there: "The ham was genuine, perhaps tasting of violets on the wishful tongue."

Yes, the restaurant, but the Gare de Lyon was more. It was Clock Tower and Big Ben Bar, café-brasserie, the newsstand, the grand stairway, Le Train Bleu. . . . It was a place through which she had traveled with her husband south to Dijon in 1929 and with her parents a decade later. In her words, "No other railroad station in the world manages so mysteriously to cloak with compassion the anguish of departure and the dubious ecstasies of return."

In fact, it was her "love affair" with the Gare de Lyon that she described to her next-door neighbor in Paris, the writer Janet Flanner, when she learned in the sixties that the then-dilapidated restaurant was doomed. Flanner in turn communicated this concern about the monument's potential demise to André Malraux, whose powers as minister of culture included decisions about when things would be officially declared *"monuments historiques."*

"He seemed to know," as she put it, "that a minor

living art form is far more vital than a major dead one."

When I asked her if she ever went back, she smiled at her recollections from the seventies of its new floors, lace curtains, refurbished walls and ceilings. She even said that the waiters smiled as if they knew the secret.

The secret? That was the thing I could never get straight. I took a last dropless sip of the *vin rouge* with a regretful sigh that I had not ordered instead a brandy and water like Mary Frances always did at the Gare de Lyon. (But then this was my trip, not hers). I pulled my sweater around me because it was getting chilly. I admitted to myself that hours of attempting to feel like Mary Frances had not given me any insights about whether she had anything to do, really, with the salvation of this great French landmark-monument-artwork called the Gare de Lyon. And I decided that when I got back to California the following week, I could come right out and ask her: "Mary Frances, I was wondering, last week when I was in Paris, seeing things like the Gare de Lyon and other historical monuments, well, I was thinking about you . . ."

"Yes?" she said, looking at me quizzically as she sipped her drink from a bent clear plastic straw. "What about it?"

I took a deep breath. This was the moment when I knew I was wrong. Now finally I had come to my senses.

Naturally I had misunderstood, put things together in the wrong order, drawn a conclusion that was preposterous, ludicrous. This soft-spoken voice, first heard in a cradle in Albion, Michigan, eight decades ago, how could it possibly have made a discernible sound against the destruction of the Gare de Lyon? But there I was, asking it.

"So, Mary Frances, did you actually save the Gare de Lyon?"

There was no hesitation. There was maybe a slight deepening of the smile at the corners of her mouth. The mobile eyebrows did not move. The face did not explode into astonishment. She said simply, "I like to think I had a hand in it."

A Realistic
Picture of Public
Transportation
in the Twentieth
Century

In the center of Harvard Square the newspaper stand looked as if it started out some years ago as a homey little pile of bricks and boards covered with a big Magritte-style black umbrella to keep out the rain. Someone may have added a small table here and there, as needed, until the whole arrangement ossified in the middle of the street and no one had the heart to tell them to move. Like so many of the wonders of Cambridge, Boston, and environs, it looked like a tradition that had become its own justification. If I had nothing else to do, I would have been more interested; but that wasn't what I had come there to investigate.

On that particular June day Harvard Square glistened with sunlight, glistened because of the summer rain that misted down every hour or so, reminding me that summer is still humid in the East even after all these years and that this sunlight is nothing like the California one to which I had become accustomed. I wandered into the newspaper shop to look for a Harvard-inscribed cup to give to my eight-year-old daughter, who collected such things. They had only big, white, oversize beer steins, which wouldn't fit on the narrow shelves of the cup case in her room. It wasn't big enough for beer steins, not then, anyway. Some other store would probably have little cups the size that I wanted. But it wasn't cups, either, that I had come there to find.

It was the morning of my first day there, the first of three days I would spend in the Schlesinger Library at Radcliffe, which holds the papers of M. F. K. Fisher. These include, according to the library's printed description, an "unprocessed collection" of photographs, drafts and galleys of books and articles, newspaper clippings, correspondence, and two motion pictures packed up in twenty-five cartons and two file boxes.

I had never done anything like that before, and I found the prospect very exciting. What might I learn, reading her thoughts as a bride in Dijon in 1929? Or her letters home from Paris or Marseille or Aix in the fifties, sixties, and seventies? Or from Piney Woods, Mississippi, where she taught in a segregated school in 1964?

"It's all there," Mary Frances had told me when I mentioned traveling to Radcliffe to go through the papers. "Anything anybody wants to know. No secrets." I remember thinking she had looked at me suspiciously as she described another person whose reasons for going to Radcliffe to read her papers were "the wrong reasons." "Scandalmonger," is how she put it; "just interested in things with shock value, the private stuff."

My explanation of just why I wanted to peruse her past was, if I was not mistaken, thereby succinctly requested; under the circumstance, my voice took on a certain stammering quality. "Oh, no. Well, I just thought, in order to have a good overview, set things straight in my mind, that I would like to spend some time with these documents. Do you think it's worth going?" It would be a big trip for me, California to Massachusetts, arrangements for my daughter, and so on. In fact, I had traveled to Paris the month before, where I had conducted a different kind of research into her life, the kind of research that involves sitting in cafés for hours trying to conjure up bygone eras and their inhabitants. There I had hoped to feel what she'd felt just being there, walking down the Champs Élysées or stopping on the Pont Neuf or writing all afternoon in the rain.

She pursed her lips and rolled her eyes, which had suddenly turned a stern gray color.

"It's up to you, dear," she said—accusingly, I thought. For some reason, I was beginning to feel guilty just looking at her.

"I'll write a letter to them, if you'd like; tell them you're coming," she volunteered, taking me by surprise. "Let me know the dates."

"It will be the middle of June probably," I told her.

At five minutes past 9:00 A.M. on a mid-June morning, coming around the corner from Harvard Square, I first saw the tidy grass, green and brilliant, that lay like a velveteen carpet in front of the Arthur and Elizabeth Schlesinger

Library. It was like approaching stage front, the proscenium, with me as the actress-scholar. Automatically I adopted the tiptoe walking technique required when passing people reading, academically, under trees. I heard my own breath between my words as I told the young woman at the desk—surely she knew these things already—who I was, what I had come for, and how I would show her the copy of the letter M. F. K. Fisher had written as soon as I found it in the overly roomy black bag into which I had stuffed every necessity. She didn't exactly say Hello. How are you? We've been looking forward to your visit. Rather, she handed me a passel of instructions, which, though printed on many sheets of pastel paper, gave no suggestion of being colorful. She waved aside my fumbling, told me to sign the book, handed me a key. When I looked confused, she nodded her head, pointed behind me to a row of lockers, and said, without really opening her mouth, "Ten."

She seemed to have an awfully dry voice for a young person, though it was hard to tell from such limited verbal intercourse. Perhaps if my locker had been eleven or even seventy-seven I might have got a wholly different impression. I tried to convince myself that she wasn't unfriendly; perhaps she was suffering from lockjaw, or majoring in ventriloquism. A glance at the blue instructions informed me I must leave in the locker my black bag and all its necessities except pencil and paper. Notebooks and folders "will be searched when you leave."

So far this didn't seem like a Mary Frances kind of place, but then I suppose hospitality is no criterion for deciding on the institution to which to leave one's papers. I walked up the staircase to the desk outside the Bonschur Reading Room.

Two oxford-shirted women were chatting and drinking coffee from Styrofoam cups. One of them handed me a manuscript-request form, and I gave her my copy of Mary Frances's letter. Her uninvolved expression changed instantly; something must have been wrong.

"Oh, if we had only known about the asbestos before five o'clock on Friday, we could have removed the cartons you needed in advance. I'm awfully sorry."

What was she talking about? I wondered, a wave of apprehension coagulating in the back of my throat. Consequently, when I tried to say the word *asbestos?* it sounded as if there were static on the line.

"Yes, well, you see, they are removing the asbestos from the tunnels." As she went on, I got the important point that I could still request the cartons I wanted (using the manuscript-request form, of course), but they could bring out only one carton at a time. It would also take "a little longer than usual," they just wanted to warn me. One hour later I was still waiting for my first carton to arrive. One precious hour of my three days. Already I felt that peculiar anxiety of the academic, measuring life in units of research time. Meanwhile I read the walls so I could tell Mary Frances that her stuff, if it ever got through the asbestos blockade, resided somewhere beyond hallways decorated with the "Declaration and Pledge of the Women of the United States Concerning Their Political Rights and

Duties," by Isabella Beecher Hooker, dated February 22, 1871. Nearby a framed copy of words from Emma Goldman's declaration, "We are not satisfied," affirms that it is not just the ballot, but freeing themselves from public opinion and condemnation that will make women "a force hitherto known in the world . . . a force of driving fire, of life giving, a creator of free men and women."

Every time the elevator opened, I looked over, hoping for my precious folders. Eventually two huffing and puffing people arrived, bent over from the weight of the long cardboard file filled to overflowing with folders. They plopped it down on a wooden desk in the Bonschur Reading Room which I then could enter, feeling like a full-fledged researcher, now that I had something to research. From over my head a brown plaque looked down—"IN MEMORY OF MARGARET POWERS BONSCHUR"—and around me everything was constructed of sturdy blond wood: desks and chairs and rolling carts and shelves laden with heavy cartons. My carton was marked MFKF, the only thing that distinguished it from the cartons of other researchers, each with its own code: COYOTE, PAULI, MURRAY.

On the walls around me a series of black and white photos was responsible for the eternal presence of Mary Garret Hay, whose many necklaces cascaded down the brocade front of her dress. The framed face of Wenona Osborne Pinkham smiled out toward the doorway despite the weight of several large floral arrangements flourishing on her wide-brimmed hat. Not far from Wenona an entire section of the wall was dominated by Carrie Chapman Catt.

The Bonschur Reading Room had an air of impeccable righteousness that I felt a strong urge to undermine. I tried to visualize Mary Frances up on these hallowed walls. If asked, she would provide a photo of herself in her purple velour jumpsuit or maybe her nubby orange cotton Mexican shirt with the wide pink strips. She would be smiling a grand smile, hoping that because of her some committee would have to be summoned into special session to settle the question of whether to admit color photographs, not to mention smiles.

But when I saw in the back of the room a stained-glass window bright with flames and wings and the name Josephine Preston Peabody, I thought I was being too harsh. I was also wasting precious time.

Slowly I pulled the lid off the first carton. I did this with a certain trepidation because Mary Frances told me once, "for years I've been putting all my papers in acid-free cartons for the Schlesinger. But all the paper today is such inferior quality, when they finally open all the boxes, everything's going to be crumbling to pieces." I was relieved to see that it wasn't. The carton was crammed with folders, and the folders were bulging with papers. I could barely fit a finger between the folders to read their labels. I worked one folder back and forth a little, afraid to pull too hard. Everything seemed so fragile. Even so, I had a hard time overcoming my natural inclination to dump the whole thing out on the floor.

Finally I managed to free the first folder. The label read "Donald Friede" followed by the dates "1945–1951."

I stared at the label as if it were telling me something. Those were the dates of their marriage, that much I already knew. Reading through the letters quickly confirmed the story of their three-week love affair. But there were more details, some of them disturbing. In May 1945 M. F. K. Fisher packed up her two-year old daughter and took the train to New York for a rest. On May 19 she married Donald Friede, about eight years her senior. His long history in the publishing world included running the publishing company of Covici-Friede, founded in 1928, which had brought out the early works of Hemingway, Faulkner, Dorothy Parker, Clifford Odets, and Radclyffe Hall. By 1945 Pascal (Pat) Covici was with Viking Press and soon became Mary Frances's editor and friend.

Possibly due to some personal and legal problems of his own, but certainly contrary to Mary Frances's inclinations, Donald Friede convinced his bride to leave New York with him and go back to live in California. His own career included a disastrous experience as a story editor in Hollywood and a stint as literary agent in San Francisco.

Friede had more solidly based plans for his new wife's future, however, ideas that often differed from her own. He urged her to concentrate on fiction, helped her apply for a Guggenheim fellowship, and convinced her to produce a novel, *Not Now but Now*, which Viking published in 1947. With his encouragement, she wrote a chiller for the *Ladies' Home Journal*, "Legend of Love," which was compared favorably with Henry James's *Turn of the Screw.* Friede also handled the negotiations for her translation of Brillat-Savarin's *Physiology of Taste.*

Reading the return addresses on the various letters from Friede was both revealing and provocative: Gladstone Hotel, 114 East 52nd Street, New York; National City Bank, 52ième avenue des Champs Élysées, Paris; 70 Irving Place, New York.

My eye caught sight of the next several folders, lettered "Eleanor Friede," and I was immediately transported back to the previous day. At her apartment in Greenwich Village I had met Eleanor Friede herself. She was a tall, handsome woman who ran a publishing company and flew a private plane between her Village house and her home in Virginia. She was Donald Friede's widow, having married him in August 1951, after his divorce from Mary Frances. She remembered vividly the day she met Mary Frances, in Hemet, California, where Mary Frances was living with her two girls and her father.

"Donald brought me to meet her. I didn't know what in the world to expect. But she was so gracious, so kind. Even so, I felt completely intimidated."

Within a few years, they became the closest of friends and have remained so.

"I call her Dote," she said. "I am family."

Dote and the girls, Anne and Kennedy, called Eleanor Squeak, because "I have no voice in the morning!" At the time when she, Donald, Mary Frances, and the girls traveled occasionally to Provence together, they named them-

selves the Five Flying Friedes. Predictably some confusion
about the dual Mrs. Friedes arose among hotel personnel.
But it would be cleared up by morning as the employees
discreetly traded notes about which rooms everyone had
taken.

The day before Eleanor had served a cold white Bordeaux in pinched ceramic cups she called *boccallino*. They
were almost identical to the ones in Mary Frances's house,
which she usually uses for her ginned Campari drink. Eleanor referred to this specialty as Mary Frances's *"moydee-
moydee,* or however you pronounce it." Then she
apologized for her "terrible French" and continued: "It's
spelled m-o-i-t-i-é; it means half and half." With the wine
she served long, bronze baguettes and a round of soft,
triple-crème cheese appropriately named Brillat-Savarin.

Suddenly I realized I wasn't sipping Bordeaux in a
Greenwich Village back garden. I was sitting seriously at
a table in the Bonschur Reading Room. I removed the first
Eleanor Friede folder, obeying all the rules: "Documents
should lie flat on the table when you read them. Do not rest
your arm, notepaper, or any other object on manuscripts.
Be sure to *maintain the order* of the papers in each folder."

After reading several years of Mary Frances's intimate
correspondence, I began to be amazed that she was ever
able to write anything else, surrounded as she was at various times by the constant, ubiquitous demands of hus-
bands, children, aging parents, visitors, relatives. Up until
then I had assumed that she went off every morning to
some quiet writing cubicle wherein words and sentences

would come into her head fully formed and in their correct position, that she had only to sit down and let them ink themselves out onto the page. But from the evidence of these letters, she juggled her womanly roles of mother, wife, daughter, and divorcée with that of artist. It was a struggle for her to set aside any time at all for "being M. F. K. Fisher" as she refers to her writing persona. No one served as her literary bodyguard, sealing her off from incursions into her creative energies. When she wasn't picking "apple sauce, graham crackers and celery from the rug," she was under pressure to write, to fulfill contracts, to meet deadlines. A single parent for all but four years of her life, she was solely responsible for the support of her children. "The only thing I know how to do besides cook and love a few people," she noted to herself, "is to write."

I could finally appreciate fully her sarcasm about the woman who envied her because she had such a wonderful hobby. "My hobby," Mary Frances said, shaking her head up and down in exasperation. "This woman thinks being M. F. K. Fisher is a hobby."

And yet there were many triumphs recounted in these letters: the publication of her Brillat-Savarin translation, the completion of the five books compiled into *The Art of Eating,* a week of hyperactivity in which she composed four articles in five days for *House Beautiful.* There was even a reference in a review of *An Alphabet for Gourmets* that characterized her in 1949 exactly as she might be described today: "completely unorthodox, both in her likes and dislikes."

Hidden among these letters was a page, perhaps a first draft, of some thoughts by Donald Friede about what his new wife, for whom food was both thoughtful and sensual, sacramental and earthly, actually ate for breakfast. "I have seen her start the day with a cold leg of Mallard duck," he disclosed with still palpable astonishment, adding that she was just as likely to prefer a dish of steaming buttered zucchini or a toasted muffin with a glass of vermouth. "And once," he added with a pride that still shone through this crinkly, yellowed, forty-five-year-old page, "she paid me the compliment of accepting one of my poached eggs." What he concluded sounded consistent with what was probably her present attitude toward breakfast, that it is "not so much a meal as a preamble to the day ahead."

In spite of the asbestos, the staff eventually brought me more cartons, and soon I was reading letters to and from Mary Frances's sister Norah, and her nephew Sean Kelly (who called Mary Frances Anti-Dote), drafts of articles, and correspondence with editors, agents, and publishers. I resisted the temptation to read folders marked "Fans" and "With Friends" because I was afraid I'd find my own letters in them and also because I was afraid I wouldn't. I was beginning to feel something new, a sense of responsibility. What are you supposed to make of these letters and papers? I heard myself asking in the far corners of my mind.

As if in reply I found a file of correspondence between Mary Frances and *Esquire* magazine's founder, Arnold Gingrich, her long-time friend and, not irrelevantly, a fly-fishing fan. He also prided himself on his virtuosity on the violin. "Oh, he was a terrible fiddler, terrible," she told me once, adding that he called her every morning as soon as he got into the office, which for him was 8:00 A.M. New York time—5:00 A.M. her time. "It was often worse," she said with a good, solid smile for her friend who died in 1976 at age seventy-two. "Sometimes he called from Paris, or from anywhere he was. He never thought about what time it was in California. I'd be answering the phone at three o'clock in the morning." Judging from this thick pile of letters, he not only called, he wrote quite often. And she wrote back.

"Thanks for settling the problem, not a serious one, of your letters," she wrote in July 1975. "They'll go in a carton to the Schlesinger, where perhaps in a few decades, some resolute researcher will wonder why I knew so much about fly fishing and never said anything. . . .

"Or, more likely, some [researcher] will suddenly realize that the correspondence hides a realistic picture of public transportation between New Jersey and New York in the 20th century, as well as detailed notes on temperature, etc."

At least now I knew what *not* to make of all this. A certain sense of comic relief descended, and I put down my pencil and walked out of the room.

"May I leave everything as it is?" I asked the woman at the desk.

"Yes, if you'll be back today," she answered.

"I'll be back in fifteen minutes," I responded, feeling that I really shouldn't stay away even that long. But I needed something, I thought, blinking my way down the stairs and recalling all too vividly yesterday's Brillat-Savarin cheese. Once outside, I found the sunshine and the freshly cut lawn almost enough. Walking through the yard I reached Brattle Street, lined with delis, cafés, and pizza places. I was attracted by an inviting-looking shop, Croissant du Jour, almost directly opposite. I ordered a cappuccino, and the man handed it to me in a Styrofoam cup with a horrible plastic top snapped on so unremovably it almost qualified as childproof. He had obviously misjudged me as a "to go" kind of person.

I set the cup on the counter behind me. Since my usual method of opening such containers—handing them over to my eight-year-old child—was not available to me, I began prying the lid off very carefully, starting at the side farthest from my yet-uncoffeed T-shirt. But when I looked up suddenly at the picture on the wall in front of me, everything stopped. It was a painting of the Café George V on the Champs Élysées, with the Arc de Triomphe looming at the end of the street. It was the very café where just a month ago I had sat for several hours trying to imagine what Mary Frances might have been doing during her days in Paris. Despite the fact that he was a bad judge of character, I was so excited I turned to the coffee man.

"It's unbelievable," I said as he set out a tray of just-baked croissants filled with spinach and Bulgarian feta cheese, a combination that struck me as unnatural though not wholly unappetizing. I explained how I was at the Café George V just weeks ago, writing about the very person whose papers I was researching right across the street. He was not unimpressed.

"You mean it's a real place in that painting?" he asked, amazed. Perhaps the owners of this place had just picked out the picture of the Café George V from a kit of wall treatments for Parisian theme cafés. Wouldn't surprise me a bit.

"Yes," I answered anyway, "and it looks just like that, except . . ."— I hesitated, examining it closely to make sure—"they've left out the Burger King next door. Oh, and I don't see the telltale golden arches down the street either. But then, this is more like wishful painting than stark truth."

I talked to him a bit more, working the edge off my amazement. I had a suspicion they wouldn't let me back into the Schlesinger Library if my adrenaline level was too high: it might cause a disturbance; someone might sense enthusiasm on the premises and lose concentration. I realized that coincidences happen in situations like this, when you're paying attention, looking for connections, trying to be entirely too alert. So I shouldn't have been surprised— but I was—when I fell into a few more coincidences during the next two days.

After an afternoon of reading randomly through Fisher's life, I decided to visit Walden Pond. I found myself thinking of them together, Mary Frances and Henry David. They are both poets of the possible, always finding strange birds, mending everyone's ways, coming to new conclusions with the same repositioned evidence, realizing, reprimanding, and wandering off again. They leave behind plenty of recommendations:

"If you would know the flavor of huckleberries, ask the cowboy or the partridge. It is a vulgar error to suppose that you have tasted huckleberries who never plucked them. . . . The ambrosial and essential part of the fruit is lost with the bloom which is rubbed off in the market cart."

Thus speaks Thoreau; but they both have a kind of sophisticated naïveté about the world, its ponds and its pastures. They are self-congratulatory about their ability to remain untempted by the vanities and deceits of progress. They are always, in some sense, alone.

"Tomatoes," she instructs, "the best way to eat them is in the garden, warm and pungent from the vine, so that one can suck unashamedly, and bend over if any of the juice escapes."

My second morning was also one of voracious reading—this time a carton of Mary Frances's letters written in the early fifties from her home in Whittier. "The ranch," she called it in descriptions of life there with her two little girls, both under age ten, and their ailing grandfather Rex, then in his seventies. It was partly because of his deteriorating health that Mary Frances, once widowed and twice divorced, returned to her hometown. Having lived everywhere from France and Switzerland, to Mexico and Hollywood, she found Whittier both a safe harbor and a millstone. The details of her daily life filled her prolific correspondence, her own personal journals, and the "invisible letters" that she wrote in her mind and in intimate notes to herself. Perhaps it is ironic that her closest brush with the family business of journalism was her work with patients at the Norwalk Hospital for the Insane, helping them write and publish a newspaper.

When I left the library for a short respite, I saw in the window of a nearby shop a beautiful blue-green scarf and decided to buy it for a friend. The proprietor, who was careful not to endanger his hard-earned reputation as an old codger, agreed to gift wrap it "only because I'm not too busy today." He asked where I was from and then told me he had visitors from California staying with him at the moment.

"They're from Whittier," he informed me to my astonishment. "That near you?"

"In a manner of speaking," I told him. When I mentioned that I was "at the very moment, right down the street, reading some forty-year-old letters written by a famous Whittier resident," he was not left breathless at the coincidence. He thought he'd heard of M. F. K. Fisher; he wasn't positive. But he was sure his friends would know her name, and so was I. I wrote it down on a piece of note paper, "M. F. K. Fisher," so he'd get it straight. I didn't know why exactly, but I felt I should, that somehow I was helping to complete a circle. Well, it couldn't hurt, and I'd never know, I thought, hurrying back to the Schlesinger.

*   *   *

The third morning I pulled into the Cambridge all-day parking lot feeling both sad and celebratory. It was my last day, my last immersion into this past world that belonged to someone else. I was a moon walker with no real right to be there, trespassing among the craters of someone else's landscape, kicking up dust in previously peaceful terrain, causing reverberations where there had been no sound. These MFKF cartons in my charge were now unsettled, they'd been invaded. An alien, however friendly, had descended upon them. And for what? For a few things I didn't know, for many things I didn't want to know, for more about what I already knew. If "it's all there. . . . No secrets," as she had told me, why was I not finding it? Why wasn't there more about the things we never talked about in person: her relationships with men; more about what she called the "very good affaire" (her personal orthography) she'd had after her husband Dillwyn's suicide in 1941; more about "another affaire" following the birth of her daughter Anne in 1942, "which lasted about 2 years"? What about the anguish of her work? The anguish was my assumption, a sine qua non I posited because she was after all a writer, so it must be there somewhere. Anger. I wanted more anger, at least more of that petty impatience to which poets and artists feel they are entitled. Envy, pride—more of the capital sins; more downright gossip. In my two days here, I had found some of these things but not many. Perhaps like most people she never expressed in correspondence her most intimate thoughts. These questions did not really bother me because, after all, it's her life; she can scatter or sequester whatever clues she chooses.

Instead of going directly to the library on the third morning, I walked into the Sage Grocery, the perfect pun for a trendy food store in the Harvard-Radcliffe community. I was attracted to the stuffed grape leaves resting in a cozy little carton. They would make a nice hors d'oeuvre at the end of the day. I bought them, along with some crunchy corn bread, and put them in my locker.

I felt a little daring. Perhaps I would dip into those fans and friends folders, just for fun. I found the right file box, marked 71-58-78-M 197 CARTON 9, and pulled out a folder. The letter on top was from Mary Frances to a San Francisco restaurant reviewer named Jack Shelton. Incredibly, it was about grape leaves. She had discovered a superior brand of stuffed grape leaves, she told him, that he should know about. In detail she described their luscious qualities as I sat there, affected by this third uncanny coincidence and by the suspicion that the grape leaves I had just bought were probably going to be kind of awful.

I settled in for the day, looking, as I had been, for nothing in particular. By the 1960s Mary Frances's daughters had progressed into full-fledged teenagers, and she had more time and more mobility for her work. With her increasing number of trips abroad, there was also an increase in her creative output. Nineteen sixty-one saw the publication of *A Cordiall Water,* her first book since *An Alphabet for Gourmets,* published twelve years earlier. She wrote *The*

Story of Wine in California in 1962 and, two years later, *Map of Another Town: A Memoir of Provence.* While researching and writing *The Cooking of Provincial France,* published in 1968, she lived in Paris and commuted to the south of France by train as a way of taking in the countryside. "Gastronomy Recalled," her regular column in *The New Yorker,* was published in 1969 as a collection, called *With Bold Knife and Fork.* After completing *Among Friends,* published in 1970, she again made several excursions to the south of France. In 1978 she published her next book, *A Considerable Town,* which is what she called Marseille.

From her notes and stories, observations and writings, much of them composed in and about France, came three more books in the 1980s: *As They Were* (1982), *Sister Age* (1983), and *Dubious Honors* (1988).

France was her catalyst, her inspiration, if not her salvation. Therefore, it was fascinating to come across, in a nearby folder, her earliest correspondence from Dijon. It was also surprisingly easy to imagine her eighty-year-old face as the shiny, smooth-cheeked face of a newlywed in France for the first time. She wrote home about the drawing lessons and German lessons she was taking, about her husband's studies in Dijon, about the flower he gave her every Thursday morning; she wrote, of course, about food, notably the lark they ordered for dinner because they thought the word meant "pheasant." Hunger and dismay inhered in her description: "When it got to the table, perched on a little square of toast, we thought it was a mushroom." I found that there were practical reasons for the accordian lessons she took when she and Al Fisher moved to the cooler climes of Strasbourg: "I had to do something to keep warm," she explained.

I even discovered that there was yet another Mary Fisher, whom she'd never mentioned to me. This one, a notorious smuggler of precious gems, had a passport photo resembling M. F. K. Fisher so closely that on three occasions Mary Frances was detained by the authorities and, in her words, "grilled behind locked doors." From her grim, detective-story tone, I was sure that she enjoyed it.

Toward the end of the day I filled out another form, the Schlesinger Library–Radcliffe College photocopy-order form. I asked for a few dozen pages that I wouldn't have time to read thoroughly. During my last hour I came across, quite by chance, a few miscellaneous papers that for no particular reason caught my eye. I seemed to have been drawn to them magically, as if this were one of the daily coincidences. The last was a letter, dated February 14, 1972, that Mary Frances had written to a friend. As I read it, I found the explanation for everything, including everything I had not found: "The people at Radcliffe (Schlesinger Library) have asked me for 'everything' for their files on American women, but there are many I prefer not to be made public property."

Backhanded Compliments

It wasn't until I got to know M. F. K. Fisher that I began to realize the possibilities and power of the backhanded compliment. I had always liked backhanded compliments, though I found them difficult to formulate, to strike the proper balance between enthusiasm and insult, ambiguity and honesty. They should also have a whiff of sarcasm, a twinkle of good-natured teasing. I thought of them as an inverted way of saying something nice.

But in the hands of M. F. K. Fisher, the backhanded compliment could be even more incisive. She needed only a few spare words, sliced off quickly and deftly placed with the speed and skill of a sushi-bar chef. Her version, more backhanded than is common to the genre, had an almost lethal beauty. Though hard to appreciate while still reeling from the impact, they were admirable recollected in tranquillity.

Thanking me for a review of *Among Friends,* she once wrote, "I agree that it is the only review that I have read to the end without wanting to throw up."

"The cuisine was good," she said about a meal at one

of San Francisco's trend-setting restaurants, whose chef had served each course atop its respective painterly sauce; "definitely the Puddle School from start to finish, but all very fresh and good *as well as* stylish." In her personal lexicon, the single word stylish, all by itself, is death.

And in reply to a piece I had written and asked her to critique, she wrote "I am undecided about whether to write a courteous letter (note) of ambiguous appreciation and thanks, or to tell you what I think of it. . . . I think I'll settle for the first alternative, and not risk your friendly feelings."

I sometimes suspected that what she had perfected was not the backhanded compliment but its opposite, whatever that may be termed. And whatever it was, I was sure I was staring at a whole paragraph full of it one day when I received a letter in which, after touching on a variety of diversionary topics, she wrote the following about *The California-American Cookbook*, a book I was writing: "Will you please tell me how the book is going? I'm much impressed that you are doing it in bits and pieces. . . . I would be scared silly by that. I've never written a book that way."

What did she mean by "bits and pieces?" And did she really want to know about my book? She certainly had at first, about a year before, when I told her about it. She seemed genuinely interested in the idea that much of the inspiration for current California "stylish" cuisine could be found in ordinary down-home American regional cooking. She had offered me her help and time; in her enthusiasm she had written me a galvanizing letter about how any library card catalog "will turn up treasures," adding that "my own shelves, which are at your full disposal, are rich." She spontaneously presented lists of writers I had already read—Helen Evans Brown, Evan Jones, Waverley Root, Raymond Sokolov—and titles and authors I'd never heard of—*Gluttons and Libertines* by Marston Bates, *The Omniverous Ape* by Lyall Watson, the early American kitchen guides of Marion Harland ("I have always been a push-over for Marion Harland"), and some "complete fascinators" like George and Berthe Herter's *Bull Cook and Authentic Historical Recipes and Practices,* which starts out, as she promised, with "How to make real corned venison, antelope, moose, bear and beef." She referred me to an article she once did about American fireless cookers, the first versions of which were really English and were called hay boxes. "In other words," she summed up in a letter to me, "I assume that I think you *should/ought/must* start working on The Book."

"I hope you'll let me write something for the book, a little preface or something, anything." She'd said it as if the decision would be mine, if I deigned to let her do it, if I would bestow upon her the honor of allowing her to contribute to my book.

If you play your cards right, Mary Frances, maybe I'll let you get a word in edgewise. But don't count on it. That's what I should have said. But instead I looked down at the floor and nodded and mumbled. It wasn't eloquent, but what it meant was, "Thank you, Mary Frances. Nothing would make me happier, nothing could be more just than to have one page of you bound in with all those pages of me, as if we were throwing a party together. After all, it's your fault that I'm in this position; it was reading your books way before I met you that got me to think of food as something more than overdone roast lamb, to think of life as something more than overdone roast lamb. I liked the way you could be anywhere doing anything, including practically nothing, and make a big fuss about it, literarily.

"Thanks" was all I had actually managed to say, but for the rest, well, I thought she knew.

Besides, who had she not written a preface for lately? She seemed to be specializing in the preface business. Not that she was doing hers in any customary or even accepted manner. She was not writing innocuous introductions, a genre characterized by fluff and puff, the proper domain of copywriters and professional press releasers. Instead, she was using the space for her own quirky observations on things, her unpredictable takes, her backhanded compliments. She found in other people's books the appropriately ironic setting for her thoughts, which often, when she was in her finest form, collided with the author's. In a book about square meals she included the definition of *square* as "anything from socially hidebound to plain stodgy." In an introduction to a collection of recipes put out by a women's association ("well-meaning females"), she did not fail to mention how *usually* books of this genre (not this one, of course) are "sad and pathetic and truly funny, . . . very bad, or rather . . . not very good . . . inept."

Her prefaces were often not what people expected or

even wanted, when it came right down to it. But she did them, and the line across the cover, "PREFACE BY M. F. K. FISHER," was always pasted on by the grateful publisher no matter what the words said. It did not seem strange when a few years later she published these forewords and afterwords and prefaces in a single volume, *Dubious Honors.* They had a life of their own; they served her iconoclastic purposes.

I liked the idea that her preface for my book would no doubt include both her approval of the California style and her scathing condemnation of any attempts to identify it, to package it up in book form. Until I received her letter about the bits and pieces, however, I had no indication of her thinking. Oh, there had been the minor uproar about the subtitle.

"Did you say, *Innovations on American Regional Dishes?*" she asked me with puzzled, frowned-over eyes.

"Yes. It's supposed to be like variations on a theme," I explained. "The idea is that current California cooking and the young chefs who are creating it are really playing with the cooking traditions from all parts of the country. This is partly because so many of them come from somewhere else."

This cogent logic did nothing to unfrown anything, but I had a well-developed argument, pages of it, to support this basic concept; it was the subject of the part of my book that I'd already written. I started babbling out bits of it, knowing I could go on and on for hours, like a well-rehearsed attorney for the defense. Why that analogy sprang to mind is inexplicable, though not irrelevant.

"Michael Field has a book," she began, looking me straight in the eyes, her face smoothing out. "Something musical, like theme and variations."

"Yes," I smiled, feeling a strange relief at having slipped out of the focus of attention. "I know that book. It's full of tasty transmogrifications of leftover turkey and cold roast beef."

"I think that's what you're trying to say, isn't it?" she asked. "Variations? You wouldn't say 'Innovations *on*'; you could say 'Innovations *with.*' But what you really mean is 'New ways with old dishes.' . . . Well, I don't know," she summed up with a sigh. "You would know better than I."

That was her only objection, some grammatical minutia in the subtitle. Hardly anything to worry about, I tried to convince myself, though I could imagine her writing an entire preface about awful subtitles. Not a bad idea, really; better not bring it up.

"I've never liked any of the titles of my own books," she confessed. "Except maybe *Not Now but Now.* The feeling is supposed to be something like if you're a parachutist in an airplane. There is a precise, single moment you're supposed to jump. It's not now, but *now!*"

I told her that the working title was of course subject to change and that I was not going to give her the manuscript until after my editor had gone over it. I didn't want her plowing through a whole bunch of stuff that might be rearranged or changed in the final version. Since she would be writing the preface, she should have in hand exactly what she was writing a preface for.

"Of course," she agreed, "I could never write anything for something I didn't know well. I hope your publisher isn't going to diddle with you. Don't let your publisher diddle with you."

This led to a nice comfortable discussion about how terrible all publishers were, for various and all reasons.

"The important thing is to write what you as a writer want to write, not what they want you to write in New York," she said, going on to damn the voracious conglomerates that had been devouring publishing houses, magazines, and newspapers.

"None of my books has ever sold," she announced proudly. "A few thousand copies, maybe; nothing much." She waited for the incredulity to set in and added enigmatically, "Poor Henry."

"Henry?" I repeated.

"My agent, Henry Volkening," she said with a nostalgic chuckle for the man with whom she worked for a quarter of a century. With the ten percent he collected representing her, he was able, she insisted, to save up enough to treat them both to a martini once a year. I took this as a metaphor, for reasons of self-protection. This can't be true, I thought to myself, conjuring up the vision of my hundreds of note cards on American regional dishes, innovations notwithstanding. After all this, can I expect nothing more than an annual drink?

"Well, things are looking up," I argued with mock optimism. "Agents are now charging fifteen percent; maybe I'll get some pretzels along with my martini."

After trading some horrifying statistics about the average income of writers and how much trash is being published and how nobody reads anything of value, we returned to the current popularity of her books.

She admitted, grudgingly, that a certain fame seemed to have set in of late, as if it were a virus. There was a nuance, in her voice, of regret, even annoyance, tempered with resignation. This too will pass away, she seemed to be saying, and then she could look forward to being underappreciated again, like every other self-respecting writer in this country. Or, like so many writers, maybe it was what she hadn't written that gnawed at her.

Like a book about childbirth and motherhood that she had once collected notes for. Or a study of Madame Juliette Récamier, the beautiful nineteenth-century French "intellectual cum sexual refugee" whose salon attracted her country's leading political and intellectual leaders. Mary Frances found Récamier so fascinating that she once signed a contract to write a book about her. She received an advance for serial rights but years later had to return it when she realized she could not complete the work. She did complete a translation of Colette's *Vagabond* that did not see publication because, at the time, there was no audience in this country for Colette, according to the prevailing "publishing wisdom," which might, we gigglingly agreed, be a contradiction in terms. And once, after teaching in a black school in Mississippi, which she called "a most shaky, shattering, extraordinary experience," she vowed, "I'll write about it some day." But she never did.

One of her ideas for a book still appeals to her. "It would be a book that puts you to sleep in three pages," she explained, laughing. "Someone could write a whole series of books like that. You may have that idea if you'd like," she offered, with a generous nod.

I thanked her, adding I hoped that my book, "when it's published, doesn't fall into that category automatically."

She told a fascinating tale about a love story between a Japanese and an American she wrote for *The Saturday Evening Post* in 1941.

"It was scheduled to come out on December 7, of all dates," she recalled, widening her bright, suede-gray eyes. "They pulled it at the last minute, of course. 'Whatever Happened to Miss Brown?' it was called."

Mary Frances once pointed to a shelf where she had grouped together books and notes for several articles she had never written. There was a bevy on gentlemen's cookery, another on gourmet diets, a surprisingly large number of dusty tomes on sexual behavior in marriage (where else?) and a clump of books on etiquette. Among the latter I found one dated 1893 and read aloud rules about never kissing in public and how you should not even consider riding your horse in front of anyone until you had gained proficiency.

These books were interspersed with the works of Robert Louis Stevenson, Boswell and Johnson, Thackeray and Freud, which I assumed were there for reasons other than their roles in gourmet diets or gentlemen's cookery.

Something jogged her memory: "As I remember, the clippings and notes for *A Cordiall Water* over some twenty years were easy to put into a big envelope that I carried around with me, not knowing when the right moment would come to pull it together. And when that moment came, everything was easy as pie, in a third-class hotel bedroom in about three months. In Aix."

Clippings and notes thrown in an envelope? But then what did she mean by that "bits and pieces" remark? Wasn't this an admission that she had, in fact, "written a book that way."

Maybe what she meant was that I was working with a co-author, which she had never done. We had divided the work according to our own strong points, my co-author creating the recipes while I handled the research and writing. Not only was it efficient, it was rewarding, and fun, to be able to do what we each liked best. Well, she'd see how well everything worked out once she got the manuscript.

When she did, she had several complaints, most of which I could not decipher. She seemed to be put off by the very massiveness of the manuscript and the profusion of colored pencil marks, arrows, and yellow stickers hanging off every other page. The thing was definitely unwieldy, difficult for her arthritic hands to hold and turn pages. I told her to forget about it until the galleys were available, even bound galleys.

One day during the next months the publishers sent me a description of my book that they were going to use to advertise its publication. It ended with the line "FORE-WORD BY M. F. K. FISHER." I looked at it a long time, thinking everything over. Then I got up, dialed the publisher, and told them to take the line out. Someone would see it and call her up, I was sure. Already I knew that that person would be the one person in America whom she didn't want knowing her business. I felt that she might get so upset by this betrayal of her plans that she might not do the preface at all.

Things moved quickly, however, and soon the publisher was able to send her the galleys and then the bound galleys. Still, nothing came back. There was some discussion about protocol: how or if to proceed, who should call whom and when. I could not deal with the situation. I was heartsick.

Finally one morning my editor called to say that this, then, was the last possible moment; the book was going to press. Much as I hated to do it, I did call Mary Frances, attempted to communicate the idea that if she was going to write something, the time was not now, but *now*. I hung up the phone, not really knowing what to expect.

The next thing I knew, I received a postcard from Mary Frances saying your editor "writes that my letter about the book got to her too late for the first-edition print-

ing but that it will be on the next one, and in a letter for
press release now. Ho hum."

Every once in a while I read over what she wrote,
which never did get bound into the book, like my imagined
invitation to a party: "a good, clear and really charming
attempt to be even younger than [the] cult [of regional
cooking] itself."

Usually I just think of it as a backhanded compliment,
a really good one; in fact, in terms of inscrutability, one of
her best. I can't imagine what I did to deserve it.

An Invitation to
M. F. K. Fisher:

Why Me?

"Y ou're crazy," announced my
friend Frances with a noticeable absence of ambiguity
when I mentioned that I had just invited Mary Frances to
lunch.

"Whatever will you serve? How can you possibly cook
an entire meal for M. F. K. Fisher?"

Good question, I thought. Two good questions, to be
exact. I'll think of something, I told myself brightly, as I
hummed the atonal little tune that comes to me in moments
of otherwise quiet desperation. Sure, I had often brought
her little treats and dishes. But I had never taken on the
responsibility of planning and executing, not to mention
serving, an intelligent succession of courses, from nibbles
and wines right on through to dessert. I knew her well
enough to appreciate that, in matters of the table, she had
a million little prejudices. I did not know her well enough
to avoid every last one of them. I decided to proceed sys-
tematically. "What does M. F. K. Fisher serve me?" I asked
myself, thinking over my dozen years of eating, off and on,
at her house. I scribbled "MF lunch" on a piece of paper,
ready to jot down any reasonable inspiration.

Suddenly I could almost smell the roasted coriander that filled the kitchen on one of my visits to Glen Ellen. I remembered walking toward her, across the licorice-black tiles of her dining room. She was saying something.

"Chicken legs" is what she was saying, "I hope you like chicken legs." She craned her neck to reach me with a welcoming kiss, adding mysteriously, "Hugs will have to wait."

As explanation, she wiggled her fingers, which were wet and shiny, almost saffron-colored, and deeply involved in some drumsticks of the same color.

"What's that?" I asked.

"Just some chutney, maybe mango or peach or something, mixed with a little Tabasco and white wine."

I watched her rubbing the chicken with this mixture. Her hands were contorted from arthritis, to which she was either oblivious or which she was willfully disregarding, as she nimbly massaged and turned and oiled the glistening flesh. I felt more relaxed just watching her. I almost forgot to ask, "Can I help?" hoping that some vestige remained of my long-ago French cooking lessons at L'École des Trois Gourmandes, run by her chums Julia Child and Simone Beck.

Before I could remind her of this all-but-forgotten expertise, she responded. "Can you open that can?" she asked unceremoniously, pointing to a tin of pearl onions. Meanwhile she scooped up a pile of shelled peas and strung them, with the tiny white onions, around the chicken. Some fresh crispy lettuce, a smear of sweet butter, a few shakes of various bottles, and it was in the oven.

"There!" she said, her eyes taking on the gray-blue color of the Sonoma sky behind her. "How about something to drink?"

This unassuming meal was lusty, delicate, and completely different from other all-in-one dinners she almost literally threw together. On one occasion, for example, she arranged snow peas, ham, and potatoes with slender slices of roasted eggplant under a bed of thickly cut tomatoes. The only constant in these meals was the way she said "There!" when she shut the oven door.

"You always make it seem too easy," I told her, explaining that when I first read her books, I thought she was trying to suggest that throwing things together correctly was simply common sense.

"That's the way you wrote about it," I continued in a complaining tone; "as if any fool would know enough to arrange transparent slips of prosciutto next to long, creamy slices of Danish caraway cheese and to paste thin rounds of baguette together with fresh, sweet butter or to see that when all you have in the refrigerator is a drawer full of miscellaneous, tattered produce, it's a salad." Maintaining my mock-carping stance, I assured her that I had learned one thing from my first encounters with her writing: that if what she was describing was common sense, I didn't have any of it.

She laughed, accepting my criticism, or whatever it was. "I don't know if it's common sense, exactly. But I've always been informal, very informal. I go through phases of things. Soups, for example. Or I make fruit compotes for a while, mixing fresh fruits with whatever I find in the cupboard: loquats or pie cherries or litchis. I evolve recipes, if you can call them that, so I can use whatever is around.

"I just hate to throw anything out," she sniffled, as if in reaction to a strong memory. "I remember doing a long run of Jansson's temptation, a Swedish potato dish I like, or I liked once. It covers a multitude of potatoes. I like oysters, of course, any old way. Always good bread and good cheese, though. Good butter. Fresh fruits and fresh vegetables. And always," she added in a cautionary tone "appropriate to the occasion."

Although this was undoubtedly a good and incontestable rule to keep in mind, it did not provide enough specific clues to what I should be making her for lunch. Maybe sandwiches would be permissible; certainly she had rustled up such plebeian grub herself, I thought, remembering a time when she was preparing a picnic to take to Saint Helena. She was meeting her old friend Marietta Voorhees, a woman then in her nineties who owned a bookstore there. I was sitting at Mary Frances's kitchen table pulling off tufts of warmed up scones and bran muffins spread with homemade "Concord Grape Jam by M. Pritchard," according to the hand-lettered label on the jar.

"Did you want to help me make these sandwiches, or what?" she asked in a double-dare-you tone that obviated the need for a reply.

In her right hand she was wielding an important-looking knife, which she applied to two long loaves of

French bread, cutting them in thirds with a force that made me put down my scone and get to work. She cut one of the big slabs in half and started pulling out the doughy insides.

"You can be in charge of the mayonnaisation of the bread," she directed, handing me the denuded crust. "Actually, why don't you put on a glub of mustard and Tabasco and mayonnaise?" she instructed, adding not too helpfully, "Different sized glubs."

On top of the glubs she directed the laying out of ham, cheese, and watercress, pausing to apologize for her excessive efficiency. "I don't mean to sound like Mother Superior, dear."

As we completed each giant-sized construction and covered it in plastic wrap, I noticed it would disappear for several minutes. When she put it back on the table, it was somehow thinner, less chunky looking. From the mischievous look on her face, I could see that she was doing something unexpected to these sandwiches. Was it, could it be . . . ?

"Are you . . . sitting on the sandwiches?" I asked, led by the evidence to this logical but unthinkable hypothesis.

"I'm flattening our lunch," she said, with a bright giggle and keeping me in her sights so she could savor my shocked reaction.

"Oh" is what I think I said, and then we were laughing about how this was simply her very literal version of a "sit-down dinner."

* * *

For the more common interpretation of sit-down dinners, she also had definite opinions. For my information, I worked their basic wisdom into my MF-lunch list.

"I like six or eight at the table, no more. At the ranch, I often had twelve at a time. It was too much, somehow, but it was family." Mary Frances lived at the ranch in Whittier when she was a young girl and later with her two young children. At both times people were always stopping by.

"We lived in the country, so people often stayed over. They didn't like to drive home at night. But when we were children, Sunday-noon dinner was our big meal of the week, especially after Grandmother died and we refused to go to Sunday school anymore. And Sunday-night supper was a great meal at our house."

"Why was that?" I asked when she paused for some reason at this obviously prefatory note. "Because I made it!" she answered with a sudden, wide grin. "Oh, everybody would do something. Father would sometimes make oyster stew or something. But usually I'd do it."

She took the opportunity to issue her complaint about being the oldest of four. She had to take on certain extra responsibilities.

"But," she added with a hate-to-admit-it grimace, "I loved doing it, the smells and good flavors. And, well, everybody in the family liked what I did."

In one of my rare excursions into the direct approach,

I initiated a conversation with the deliberate rhetorical question "It's such a problem knowing what to serve people, isn't it, Mary Frances?"

She agreed that lately it was getting more and more ridiculous to invite people to dinner. They don't accept—or even refuse—graciously, we grumbled to each other; instead, they counter with a long recitation of things they don't eat and, even worse, why. She shook her head impatiently.

"Oh, I never pay any attention to that. They should either go away or not come at all. Or keep quiet about it. Besides, they can always find something to eat. If I want to, without any fuss, I can serve ten different meals to ten different people."

"I always write for one person," she has said, "and while I'm writing, I think of that person." She seemed to feel the same way about cooking.

"You want to please people, cook toward their tastes. I can't imagine cooking for people who don't appreciate it, or care."

She sighed a long sigh, and I knew what she meant by it: these rules we make about how we'll conduct our lives, they're always very nice and tidy and completely unworkable when applied to real people. Especially people we like. She once invited a man whom she knew quite well for a special dinner of rabbit.

"Turns out he's put off by rabbit," she explained. "This rabbit syndrome is hard to crack! Probably if I'd told him that it was a special food that had to be ordered far in advance and that it costs more than filet mignon, he would have loved it. Especially if I'd used the German word instead of that dreadful *r* word."

With my still-sparse MF-lunch list at my fingertips, I thumbed through Hal Bieler's *Food Is Your Best Medicine,* a book she had once given me. Maybe it would contain some clues to her special preferences. I knew she distributed this book to her friends and that Bieler had delivered both her babies and offered advice and help whenever she asked. To Bieler she had dedicated *An Alphabet for Gourmets* because he "taught me more than he meant to about the pleasures of the table." But I didn't learn anything much myself, so I decided to come right out and ask.

"Is there anything that you particularly like, or any cookbook that makes you salivate just thinking of it?" I inquired, hoping to locate something she truly craved, complete with instructions and everything.

A straight answer, I could tell from the upturned position of her lips, was not what I was about to get.

"I rather like that one there," she said, indicating a white-jacketed book with a drawing of a mangy-looking creature holding a tree branch and stirring something in a vat. It was a collection of witches' recipes called *Caldron Cookery: An Authentic Guide for Coven Connoisseurs.* I opened it to the category "Fiesta Favorites and Specialties" and found several unlikely recipes not to add to my lunch plans: "To Make a Woman's Hair Fall Out," "To Make Men Appear Headless," "To Cause a Man to Go Insane." By far the shortest was "To Foretell the Future (I)." It was followed, predictably, by "To Foretell the Future (II)." The recipe required a single ingredient, "1 weasel," and the preparation couldn't have been easier: "Eat the heart of the weasel while the vessel is yet panting, and you can foretell the future."

"One interesting thing about witches," I heard Mary Frances comment, "is how hungry they always are."

I looked over at her with one eye, to see if she was at all serious about this. My other eye led me back to the receipt for "Love Charm," which required doing something to the genitals of a wolf that I knew I didn't want to do, much less think about.

I decided to switch the subject to desserts, the one course she treats nonchalantly though not carelessly.

"I admire desserts, and I like them, but I never did much about them, really. Sometimes I would make cookies or something. When we were kids, every Saturday morning mother would come down to the kitchen and make a big cake."

"For the weekend?" I asked, wondering just how big a cake it was for four dessert-starved children.

"Oh, no. It would be gone in five minutes," she said, laughing.

Though I still had no idea what I might make her for lunch, I did have a scheme for dessert. I'd steal her trick of scooping vanilla ice cream into a bowl and crumbling amaretto cookies on top. Or maybe I should follow the recipe Mary Frances once gave me for something called iced cream:

  1 cup sour cream
  ½ cup coarse brown sugar
  ¼ cup kirsch, rum or brandy
Beat cream and sugar together until smooth. Add
liquor, mix well, and freeze. Serve on hot compote
or *tarte*.

She did not refer to these instructions as a recipe but, rather, as an "excellent trick." It is typical of her response to requests for how to duplicate a specific taste or dish.

"Of course, they asked me for the recipe," she once wrote to me about a soup I had made for her, which she had served to "two of my fussiest friends." Since they assumed that she had made it herself, she wrote, "I lied a bit here and there, but probably gave them a fairly decent version of your little masterpiece. To cover everything, of course, I added that it was different every time. This useful gambit is a godsend, and in case you don't already know it, I pass it along to you with my blessings."

Some of her recipes really *were* tricks, as I discovered one day, glancing at a scribble of instructions. It read: "soup of 2 parts Campbell's potato to 1 part Campbell's cheddar—dash of sherry—very good."

No. Not me. She could get away with that; I could imagine her appreciative guests telling her how sumptuous the soup was and asking, perchance, "What is that wonderful little taste?" "It's the sherry," she might answer. "Ah," they would nod, "of course." Or she might say, "It's just based on one of those old peasant potato soups into which you throw some cheese or bread or whatever else you might have around." Or she might come right out and tell them: "Good old Campbell's. Sometimes they're not so bad." And they would laugh and raise their wine glasses to toast her sense of humor and never believe it, not in a million years. But I wasn't going to attempt anything quite that daring with her as my lunch guest.

Not that she was pretentious, exactly. In fact, she had a penchant for reverse snobbery that was maddening. There were, for example, the two food gifts I had recently brought her, an elegant eggplant caviar made with roasted vegetables blended with herbs and spices, plus a big, over-size can of potato chips (a little joke). In her immediate thank-you note she wrote that she hoped I would come up soon and share the "eggplant mish mash [which] will still be here"; as for the potato chips: "I doubt that they will last until the next date."

I reminded myself, however, that there were some foods about which Mary Frances had unswerving opinions. I had decided that the Swiss chard from my own home garden was a definite "yes" until she said, "I don't know why anyone would bother." Parsnips? "I could never get interested in them." Goat cheese? "It often tastes like dirt to me." Rutabaga? "Down with it." Baby carrots? "All those prissy vegetables have no taste, anyway." Okra? "I wouldn't waste it on just anybody." What about Veuve Clicquot Rosé? "It's just a fancy pink champagne." And truffles? "Ah, well, and ho hum. But they are fun to *read* about." And did she ever have tripe? "Oh, often, often. Any old way at all. I love it." Potatoes? "Mashed. The first time I tasted them, really tasted them, was at a little restaurant in France, the Hostellerie de la Poste in Avallon. They were spilling with butter and served as a separate course. They made me realize what food could be. And raw potatoes were very good, too, at least one time in my life." Raw potatoes? "As children, we were told never to eat raw potatoes. They were supposed to be poison. But one day we went down to the basement of my friend Eleanor's house, cut up a potato, and passed it around. Perhaps that was the best meal I ever ate."

I suspected that since raw potatoes no longer represented forbidden fruit, the thrill of eating them was probably gone. I scratched raw potatoes from my MF-lunch list. It wasn't the foods Mary Frances served that made an event of practically everything she did. It was her sense of ceremony, the moments before eating anything, watching her rub the chicken. It was the first sizzle, the surprise of sun-yellow cornbread in a black iron skillet, the way the room filled with smells of sweet onions caramelizing. It was symphonic. There was a time for grace notes and a time for the band to play. The whole thing made you feel good: that was the point.

And maybe, sometimes, wine had something to do with it.

"We always had good wine," she said, as if she were dropping her handkerchief: a word to the wise.

"Even as a kid?"

"Sure. At the dinner table."

"Were both your parents interested in wine?" I asked.

"No. Neither one of them was. We just had it as part of our food. I was a typical prohibition child. We could get away with murder because we were not Quakers."

And what did she think about the current emphasis on pairing food and wine?

"It's essential. It's part of life. I can't see all the fuss about it. In Bordeaux the husband picks the wine, and the wife cooks to go with it. It's always been that way." She attacks the idea of a new vocabulary for these pairings: sauces that are "wine-friendly," certain meats being excellent "carriers" for certain wines.

"Of course there have always been ignorant snobs. That's part of the modern cult. They were pairing food and wine way back when, the Greeks and the Romans."

I wanted to ask her directly what she would do if she herself were planning a little celebratory meal. And yet I knew it was not a fair question, not anymore. Over the twelve years we've known each other, things have changed for her socially. Her arthritis and Parkinson's, cataracts and hip operations have curtailed her kitchen activities as well as her writing. She no longer cooks for herself.

"I don't feel at all good about it," she said, her voice a bit dry with disappointment. "I am by nature very hospitable. I was always telling people to stay for lunch, stay for supper. I keep forgetting that I can't do it. I did it very easily; I can invent things. It's fun. It's one of the terrible things about not being in control of your home, about aging. I miss it. I really do."

And yet she is often surrounded by wonderful treats that her friends and visitors send and bring her. "The ravens," she calls them, her eyes squeaking into a smile. "The food ravens always bring me food." I have seen it countless times: a car drives up, someone drops off an eggplant frittata or something, waves at her through the window, and leaves. Once she served me a luscious fresh-fruit chutney from a recipe in Claudia Roden's *Everything Tastes Better Outdoors*. I was about to ask her whether she'd made it when she said, "Claudia brought that to me when she was here the other day."

During holiday season, her kitchen-dining-living room is always littered with goodies: Belgian chocolates in the shape of miniature fans; a gilded Tahitian vanilla bean; a miniature *panettone;* a ready-to-bake *focaccia* with rosemary; a box of five-minute polenta; a small aluminum-wrapped fruitcake; a carton of what she called Amherst cookies, because of something about the people who sent them; oversize oatmeal ovals; peanut-butter cookies dipped in chocolate; leaden-looking *palmiers;* a dark-chocolate collage that tasted like rice crispies; one plain cookie in the shape of a dog; a pinwheel cookie of alternating chocolate and vanilla; a carving of two heads of angels that looked like white sugar but wasn't; a bowl of fruit, including avocados and Mexican onyx mangos; a box of Harry and David pears; a bottle of Veuve Clicquot Rosé from someone who didn't know any better; and once, a dried-out lizard that had crawled under the couch and starved to death. She called him Rodney and said he was slotted for cremation soon. There was also a Swiss-chocolate Santa Claus. "Shall we knock him down on the table and crack him open?" she asked. But we didn't.

She claims to have no interest in traditional holiday meals and entertaining, but her parties were no less festive for it. One invitation I received was a xeroxed page with this message:

Do you feel APPREHENSIVE?
Are you JITTERY?
Do lurking psychosomatic JANGLES haunt you?

———————————

The BLAHS-DE-NOEL SYNDROME can be DANGEROUS!
Treat it soon! Catch it before it catches YOU!
Symptoms: stomachic and facial yawns, repressed familial
mania with homicidal fantasies, ennui (boredom).

———————————

For temporary relief: consult local representative
of Christmas Compassion Company, Ink.,
on December 25, 1984, between 4 and 7 P.M.,
at 13935 Sonoma Highway, Glen Ellen.
— Mary Frances C. C. C.

Although I seemed to be adding nothing in the way of helpful hints to my MF-lunch list, she was reminded of another Christmas event she orchestrated some twenty years ago, which remained, like most things, still vivid in her mind. Why?

"I almost killed off my whole family," she admitted,

allowing herself a little guffaw because it was so long ago now.

"It happened on Christmas Eve or Christmas night. We all had indulged ourselves in the beautiful roast turkey, a pretty feast it was in every way. But three hours later the boat began to rock. I ran around getting samples of everything, but I knew they were all going to die."

"Did you call the doctor?" I asked.

"I didn't see any point in that; I thought they were all dead. This was in Saint Helena, in my three-story house with toilets everywhere, all of them going all night long. I did actually call the doctor in the morning and told him everyone was sleeping. He said not to worry; they were obviously not going to die. Just give them dry toast and weak tea."

"What caused it, do you know?"

"Oh, yes! I caused it! To save time I planned to stuff the turkey at night and roast it the next day. I don't know what I was thinking of. I made a stuffing of raw oysters, which I chopped into the warm dressing and stuffed into the turkey. I perched the turkey on the back porch, and during the night the weather got very balmy, the perfect environment for mass murder, pure poison. My friend Eleanor Friede said she could imagine the headlines: 'NOTED GOURMET DOES IN FAMILY.' She told me we had to be careful no one ever found out."

"And what did you say to that?" I asked, feeling free to chortle about this near disaster since Mary Frances was doing just that.

"I said that I thought no secret should be made of it."

This revelation effectively ended my dilemma about what to serve Mary Frances. Whatever I came up with, I was sure I wouldn't kill anybody. What more could she ask?

EPILOGUE: SHUT UP AND EAT YOUR TOURANGELLE D'ASPERGES

When Mary Frances finally did come to lunch at my house, I served a simple, thrown-together sort of meal.

—Oh, that, Mary Frances? Just some soup I boiled up this morning with—what was it I tossed in there?—ah, yes, asparagus. Happened to have some five-dollar-a-pound asparagus lying in the vegetable bin. The recipe, by the way—not that I bothered to follow it, really—is from Simca's book. You know, Simone Beck, your good friend?

As for the main course, Mary Frances, I didn't give it much thought beforehand, so I just mixed together what I had on hand: a few bunches of fresh baby leeks, some alderwood-smoked chinook salmon, a batch of homemade roasted red pepper fettuccine that I had planned to crank out at dawn today anyway. By chance, I was standing around the kitchen this morning rolling out these black pepper and red onion flatbreads you might like to try. No big thing, Mary Frances. And I hope you weren't looking forward to dessert today, because I really didn't get very far in that department. If you don't care for these orange pecan thins—yes, they are still warm from the oven, come to think of it—you might like a slice of the rum poppyseed cake. No, I didn't bake it special. I just happened to be doing some research on the poppyseed recipes of the Nebraska Czechs, in the course of which I went to the store and stumbled over a big box of poppyseeds and a bottle of rum; the cake sort of made itself.

As for the wines—the Trimbach Pinot blanc and Gewürztraminer—well, I met with this distinguished gentleman from the Trimbach winery. It's in Alsace; yes, I was pretty sure you would know that. And I also thought, since you had lived in Strasbourg, there might be some nostalgia element, as well as the fact that the man said he was sure you would like these two particular "years," as he put it. Of course, you're right: he would say that, being from the winery and all. Actually, if you'd rather have your pink drink with the gin and Campari, it makes no difference to me, Mary Frances. I could care less.

This MF lunch, which did include everything described (plus some preprandial almonds), took place on a Friday, the day after Thanksgiving. Mary Frances came down from the Stanford Court Hotel, where she was spending the holiday weekend. She seemed to enjoy the meal, remarking on it favorably several times during the afternoon. As she was leaving, she said it was just the right kind of meal for the day after Thanksgiving. I didn't know exactly what she meant by that, so I didn't ask.

The Art of
Art

"Mary Frances will be right with you," announced Nina, Mary Frances's nurse, who said everything as though she were still smack dab in the middle of Texas.

"Good. Thanks, Nina." I skipped down the three steps to wait in the living room, where I hoped we would be meeting today. Lately most of our visits had taken place in Mary Frances's bedroom, and although I had finally gotten over the strangeness I used to feel tiptoeing around her bedroom, I still felt more comfortable in the living room. Or more normal. I wanted it to be more normal, more like before. But those three steps had been a big part of the problem now that Mary Frances was so dependent on her wheelchair for mobility. They were perhaps the only flaw in this house so carefully tailored to the Mary Frances who moved in twenty years before.

The living room looked exactly the same as the last time, disturbingly so, in fact. It was full of a passive, dusty quiet, as if no one was spending any time there anymore. It reminded me of my grandparents' living room, closed off

behind curtained, wood-framed, glass doors to keep everyone safely away from the "good" furniture. No one ever
went near the black lacquered cane-seated chair or the
mirror-bright table or the lustrous piano. It was like a mu-
seum, though less visited. After my grandmother died, I sat
in the beautiful, black chair for about one second, and then
the brittle, dried-out seat shattered into a million pieces.

Now while I waited in Mary Frances's living room, I
sized up the chairs, and though I didn't see any cane-seated
ones, I decided to stand anyway. I liked wandering around
the house, because if you knew where to look, there were
little clues to what Mary Frances had been up to since the
last visit. She changed things constantly: the posters on the
walls, the paintings, the knicknacks on the windowsills, her
refrigerator art, of which she had possibly the world's most
estimable collection. Except for the door handles, the entire surface was a mass of children's art projects: finger
paintings, paper plates splotched with colors and glitter,
watercolors of rainbows, and drawings of witches. In small
ways she was always rearranging just about everything in
the house; it was a means of controlling her surroundings,
altering it to suit her involvements or current moods,
which one could feel simply by walking through. But lately
I had begun to think of it as her way of moving. Once her
mobility started to become curtailed, she could no longer
pick up everything and move on or plan an impromptu trip
to Aix. Yet like that of many creators, her spirit was ani-
mated by the unexpected, stimulated and recharged by ex-

otic battles and new environments. Changing the walls was not so much an extension of how she was feeling as a method of fomenting something she wasn't.

Even when she could not physically handle the canvases and objects around her, she had her ways of getting the periodic changes taken care of. More than once I was one of her ways. That was how I discovered what was behind the narrow, odd-shaped door in the living room, her "art closet" as I came to know it, for better or for worse. In it she kept her collection of paintings, many of them completed a half century ago by her husband, the artist Dillwyn Parrish. There was a Parrish turkey, a whimsical Parrish portrait of a man eating, some Parrish apples and bananas, plus a Victorian-looking house and a non-Parrish painting of Colorado that reminded her of "early O'Keeffe." Whenever I stooped down and squeezed into the miniature art closet, I felt like a claustrophobic Alice in Wonderland, expecting March Hares to pop out or a giant deck of cards to charge past me into the room.

I had also been enlisted once to rotate the posters in the house (in fact, I had volunteered), but only after she assured me that the posters were not kept in the same dreaded closet. Even a veteran house thief would have trouble locating her poster collection, which she stores, safe and flat and sound, under the rug. The posters are about everything: art exhibits, cafés and hill towns, about wine and grapes and food. Once when she tired of her favorite old Cézanne poster, I was instructed to pull the other posters out and hold them up one by one: "no, no" for the one of the *Sotheby's World Wine Encyclopedia;* "not today" for the fourth anniversary of Square One; "what else is there?" for most of the rest. Finally she settled on the one of the Musée d'Albi by Toulouse-Lautrec.

"Do you know that place?" she asked me as I tacked it to the back of the door. "It's an old brick building north of Montpellier, where they have the truffles." She went on to explain that the people who sell the truffles thereabouts also carry in their pockets some salt and some cayenne. What you do, she described, is peel the truffle and sprinkle it with pink salt and eat it.

"How do you know these things, Mary Frances?" I asked, thinking that's what these stimuli do: they bring up past events, places, and experiences. A mere glance at a poster, and a fable spins off the tip of her tongue: how the French tore up the rice they used to grow in La Camargue and planted wine grapes instead; or how the English who used to go to Switzerland for TB cures when she lived there had planted the hillsides with buttercups, but the cows ate them, and that made the Gruyère cheese bitter, and after that there was a bounty offered for the roots of buttercup plants; or how water hibiscus planted on the sides of Lake Merritt in Oakland cause some kind of awful ecological imbalance.

Today as I waited in the living room, Cézanne was in his old position. Even the slight tear at the corner was not a new one. Nobody had bothered to patch it up; maybe nobody would. Nobody had opened the Matisse book either, at least not today. Because it was so enormous, she kept the volume on a stand of its own, the way some people keep a Bible or an unabridged Webster's. She usually changed the picture every day, thumbing through the mammoth pages until she found just the right stained-glass window from the chapel at Vence, or whatever felt right. I had no trouble convincing myself that you could feel bubbly emanations from the Matisse *du jour* all through the room. When the book was closed, you couldn't feel them. I couldn't feel them today.

I lowered myself, ever so gently, onto the miniature footstool so I could peek at the contents of the coffee table. It was always smothered with books and bound galleys and literary publications, whatever Mary Frances was reading or working on. Topics ranged from rattlesnakes, herbal cosmetics, and cooking to De Quincy's *Confessions of an English Opium Eater*, *The Ellery Queen Japanese Golden Dozen*, Charlotte Painter's *Who Made the Lamb*, Katharine Hepburn's *The Making of* The African Queen, *or*, *How I Went to Africa with Bogart, Bacall and Huston and Almost Lost My Mind*, *The Fables of Mkhitar Gosh*, and Henry Miller's *Hamlet Letters* ("Very boring," remarked Mary Frances last time; "I think it was his dissertation"). Today's selection was much too neat, as though it really wasn't being picked from or added to. I wasn't sure, but it seemed that the whole stack differed little from the last time I was here, confirmation that Mary Frances had not been poking around in here. Presiding imperiously underneath the table, as ever, was Samuel Johnson's dictionary.

In the corner, next to the woodpile and the miniature

footstool with its needlepoint cover, stood the old black globe. Instead of the conventional geographic displays of lands and seas, this globe, created by her friend Gloria Stuart, was a collage of drawings and clipped pictures that was supposed to represent Mary Frances. Everything on it meant something about her, though I could never figure out what. There was a parrot, a cowboy belt on which was written *"honi soit qui mal y pense,"* a jar of honey with a bee stuck on it, a drawing of a perfectly ordered dinner table captioned "METHOD OF SETTING A TABLE IN AMERICA." Whatever it meant, it was at least a way for Mary Frances to keep her presence in this room.

Yet there was also something new in the room. I sensed it before I saw it, but then finally I noticed the refrigerator. The art-covered doors had always contributed an air of the colorful and the carefree. Now the doors were almost barren. I couldn't understand it. Why would she take down the children's art? Or did someone else do it?

"Yoo-hoo. Y'all can go in now." The Texas syllables rolled through the air.

"Oh, Nina," I said, caught off guard. "But I thought Mary Frances was coming down."

"No," she said with a regretful shake of the head. "Not today."

"See y'all later," Nina called, disappearing into her own room. I decided to check the bathroom on my way, to see whether all the "necks" were still in place. If there was one room that Mary Frances left her unmistakable imprint on, it was the bathroom. The lighting was soft, sultry even, imparting a coaxing, French-whorehouse quality. This was accentuated by the piles of plush towels and the long-armed plants and the bouquet of lipsticks beckoning from an abalone shell. The walls were always full of art: flowers, still lifes, and country walks. But a while ago Mary Frances had pulled out from the art closet all her drawings and paintings of the backs of people's heads and had them hung, floor to ceiling, throughout the bathroom. There was something funny about them, these portraits of people ignoring you completely. I smiled at the one sinuous swanlike neck I recognized: the one of the young Mary Frances, wife of the painter Parrish.

I tried to envision what she must have been like in her younger, hobnobbing years. To walk into a room and find Mary Frances, her radiating wit and style, her steel-trap mind and memory, her opinions. Not only was she a beauty, which can be easily appreciated from her photographs, but she was a force, a magnet, a holy terror.

"I was scared to death of meeting her," someone once told me about their first encounter in the early fifties; "she was such a perfectionist in her writing. Everyone knew her from *The New Yorker.*" Arnold Gingrich called her the "wizard of Saint Helena," and described her smile as "pure sunshine." She had what Pat Covici, her editor at Viking, termed an "infinite and delicately acid wisdom." New York publisher Donald Friede considered her a "major talent" and one of the literary world's "most truly creative people." As her third husband he also came to feel that she was the "damnedest combination of patsy and mulelike stubbornness I have ever known," which did not stop him from assessing her as "magnificent—as a wife, as a woman, as a mother, as a daughter, as a friend, as a mind, as a writer, as, in fact, anything."

Looking at her these days, I had no trouble imagining any of it. Her face, even her hesitating movements, still conveyed no less of that uncamouflaged sensuality, that intensity. Not everyone is drawn to her, of course; but then, that is the nature of magnets.

"Mary Frances," I called as I approached her bedroom, "are you, as they say, decent?"

"Come on in," she answered softly. Her voice, which often faded out unexpectedly and without warning, sounded normal at the moment. "Could you maybe help me a minute?"

"Oh, God, Mary Frances," I gasped when I turned the corner and saw her trying to push herself out of the wheelchair and onto the bed.

"Nina gets very nervous when I do this," she informed me, her voice shallow but breathy with irrepressible naughtiness.

"I can see why," I sighed, taking her arm and moving with her as best I could.

She told me she had fallen again and had to go to the hospital to have her artificial hip maneuvered back into position. When she saw how horrified I was, she tried to jolly the subject by talking about falling in general and how good she is at it.

When she begins to fall, as she describes it, she is able

to calm herself and even direct where she will land and on what part of her fragile anatomy. "Something I learned in college. Of course, I don't know how Rex felt about spending all that money on my college education just so I could learn how to fall skillfully all over the place."

When I persisted in looking concerned, she went on to recount her "favorite fall," something that happened a few years ago when Raymond Sokolov came to visit. After some juggling of wine and glasses and a big vase of flowers, everything came crashing to the floor, including her.

"I must say" she concluded, almost gurgling with delight, "I felt pretty comfortable sitting there in all that good red wine."

"Anyway, you look great," I said, examining her freshly rouged cheeks as she snuggled back into the propped-up pillows. This new bed she'd bought, a hospital bed with switches and hand controls and a mattress that was as flexible as a gymnast—she could move it up, down, or sideways at her feet or head or anywhere in between. She often surprised her unsuspecting visitors by changing her position when they turned away; when they turned back to her they found themselves talking to her raised knees.

It had become her world, this bed and this room. This was the space and environment that was available for her arranging and rearranging. Her universe was condensed within this perimeter. I noticed in the corner the eroded old painting of Ursula von Ott that she had bought in a

Zurich junk shop in 1936 and that became the inspiration for *Sister Age*.

"Could you turn on the light in the alcove, dear?" she asked, and I walked over there, searching for the switch. "Those are some of Timmy's watercolors," she said. "I love them because they look so wet, as if the paint is still dripping."

It made me feel sad that she couldn't easily do this herself, reach this switch so she could see the watercolors. Then I remembered the refrigerator.

"What happened to all the children's artwork on the refrigerator, Mary Frances?"

"Nothing happened to it," she answered, a bit wistfully. "I still have it all. But I had to buy a new refrigerator. When I moved in here twenty years ago," she mused, mapping out the room both with her hands and her eyes, "everything was new. I never thought I'd ever have to replace anything. I never thought . . . I would live that long."

"Well you showed them," I said, trying to spin some frivolity into a reverie I could not otherwise handle. I wanted to ask her whether she was going to put the kids' stuff back, but I didn't want to hear that she wasn't going to bother. Why put it out there, I didn't want to hear, when I'm hardly ever out of this room?

I began to notice the things that were literally closest to her, the things she'd arranged within reaching distance. These were obviously the objects and belongings she wanted to be surrounded by and to control. On the shelf beside her, which looked a little like an altar, were four gilded wooden statues that looked like the Virgin and the Magi.

There was also a conical-shaped basket, a brown pottery jug spilling over with pencils and pens, a miniature chest of drawers that might store the pierced earrings she always wears. There were also three chocolate mice for three of her children friends, stained-glass birds, blue glass jars, and a straw Jewish star suspended overhead. Nearby hung a mobile of cutouts that looked like moons and bats and things that might "go bump in the night."

But perhaps the mood was set in that cozy corner by a Chagall poster that said "VENCE—CITÉ DES ARTS ET DES FLEURS" while two people in love floated off to the left over a lot of miscellaneous flowers. She keeps things forever, I thought as I remembered her description of buying a poster in the fifties, when she and her daughters were living in Aix. I asked her if this were the one.

"Yes, I bought this one from Brondino." she said, as if it happened yesterday afternoon.

Absentmindedly I picked up a beautiful silver bell resting on her table, a graceful, elegant shape richly ornamented and brightly polished. It also seemed, on some subliminal level, vaguely familiar. It was carved with the four apostles, Matthew, Mark, Luke, and John, and although it made a sweet, tinkly sound, it was resonant and self-assured and unhesitating.

"That was Grandmother Holbrook's," she explained, adding that it wasn't her grandmother but her mother,

Edith, who made the most use of it. "Mother used to ring it when she took to her bed, usually after the birth of one of the children. And usually I would answer it." She was still mad about that; you could tell.

"I remember," I said, smiling enigmatically. "I remember reading about it, I mean. But what is this sign, 'TODAY IS'? It looks like a little blackboard."

It was from the hospital, she told me, from the last time she was there. Every day they would change the date or write a memo on it. "I took it home partly because I thought it would be a good title for a book," she said.

"You called, Lady?"

We both looked toward the doorway to see Nina standing there dressed in a denim jumpsuit with a red belt at her waist and a big smile on her face.

"Oh, Nina, I'm sorry," Mary Frances apologized. "We were just playing with the toys. Don't pay any attention."

Suddenly I realized that I was the culprit. I had bungled the flawless system Mary Frances had devised to assure herself the balance of privacy and occasional assistance that meant her very survival, psychological and physical. It did not depend on electronic gizmos or flashing lights or video surveillance. It depended on the small, bright, long-ago song that was still being sung by Grandmother Holbrook's silver bell. Mary Frances could ring it whenever she wanted. Now it was hers. Finally.

A Stew
or a Story

I had known her for years already, this amazing, outrageous, not-as-sweet-as-she-looks, unpredictable, brilliant, erratic, exasperating woman named, by her own hand, M. F. K. Fisher. So I should not have been surprised at anything, especially at surprise itself, because that is what she is so excruciatingly good at. But even I was not prepared for her unexpected invitation to look over her fascinating collection of cookbooks and "take whatever you want."

"Come up some afternoon," she whispered into the phone in a voice a bit soft and warbly and almost inaudible; "look through the books; stay for dinner. We can pull out the couch in the hallway that makes into a bed, and you can sleep over. Maybe the cats won't bother you too much."

I went up anyway on a lovely sunny Thursday, and we had some hazelnut-crescent cookies that she'd made from Angelo Pellegrini's wife's recipe—no food at Mary Frances's is ever anonymous—served with "Bert Greene's Grandmother's Famous Secret Concord Grape Jam, 1982, MFKF" labeled exactly that way and printed in the unmistakable, scratch-away handwriting of MFKF herself.

Later we dipped warm, crisp tortilla triangles into piquant salsa, both fresh from some nouveau-southwestern place in downtown Glen Ellen, and we nibbled on some leftover wild boar brought by one of the previous days' visitors (not too previous, I found myself hoping) accompanied by the Sonoma French Bakery's crusty caraway sourdough bread and a satin white brick of Mr. Vella's sweet butter.

When it finally got too late to see, I climbed onto the couch with the cats—or maybe it was only one cat, very ubiquitous—and forgot about books until morning. Her Friday schedule of visitors wasn't due to commence till noon, so I carefully scanned the endless floor-to-ceiling bookcases that line every wall of her house. Before the twelve-o'clock lunch gong, I was packing up a cardboard carton of the books she was giving me, or maybe just lending me. I was not quite sure, and the reason I was not sure was that she does not like it if you're sure. If I had said, "Thank you for giving me these books," she would have looked at me inquisitively, as if I had suddenly gone completely off balance, and said, "Yes, dear, well you keep them as long as you need them. And then when I want them back, I'll know where they are." And if I had said, "Thank you for lending me these books," I might have been felled by the other look I am much too familiar with, a half glance with raised eyebrow followed closely by an uplifted chin, a delicate sniff at the air, and what can only be called a good scolding: "Lend you? Do you think I'd have you picking through these cobwebby old books and dragging them hours and hours and miles and miles just for temporary safekeeping? Please. I only hope you get some use out of the dusty old things. And maybe a good story." So I just said thank you and came home with the books; her books, I continue to think of them, just in case.

One rainy day I stacked a pile of them beside me as I sat in bed pampered with pillows and with a steamy, morning-strong espresso. There was *How to Use a Chafing Dish*, published in 1894; *The Receipt Book of Mrs. Ann Blencowe, A.D. 1694*, more recently reissued in MCMXXV; and *Nelson's Home Comforts*, which, though it had no date, promised on the very first page that its contents "may be obtained from grocers, chemists, Italian warehousemen etc. throughout the World."

But the first book that truly caught my attention was *Things My Mother Used to Make* by Lydia Maria Gurney, subtitled *A Collection of Old Time Recipes, Some Nearly One Hundred Years Old and Never Published Before*. Because it was dated 1922, when Mary Frances was only fourteen, I assumed this was not a book she had with her all her life but, rather, a good find at a library sale in some place like Saint Helena, where she lived in the fifties and sixties. Inside the front cover, in a florid hand, a name had been written in pencil but vigorously erased. Holding the book sideways, I could make out "Florence H. Gaylord. May 1922."

The book fell open to a page containing a torn-off scrap of paper, yellowed and brittle, on which Mary

Frances had once scribbled "little judgment!" On the page was the author's foreword: "These recipes and Household Hints are written very plainly, for those who have had no experience, no practice and possibly have little judgment." Oh, yes, Mary Frances must have liked this book immediately, for if nothing else, its refreshing ignorance of modern-day PR. Today's cookbook author would be writing this book for those who have no time because they are running the family business instead of the family. There would be flattery and euphemisms for this busy, world-occupied, multitalented lousy cook. But not for the likes of Mary Frances. She would get right to the heart of the matter: "little judgment!" There's the rub. To my delight, I noticed other bits of paper poking out from where she had tucked them in, God knows when. I couldn't wait to uncurl the little notes, to be privy to the reactions and editorial comments that she had once written, intended for her eyes only.

No one there now but us two, Mary Frances and me, thumbing through this book together, a few decades apart. Would I discover anything about her, reading her notes? Some secret, a surprise she hadn't intended? Or maybe I shouldn't be reading these notes at all. I could call her and ask, "Is it all right if I read the slips of paper sticking out of one of the books I brought home the other day?" No, I decided, coming to my senses. I preferred the bother of the minor guilt I was feeling to the grand uncertainty of her reply.

My fingers fumbled for the second scrap, on which she

had written the enigmatic words "If eaten cold. . . ." I searched the page for the rest of the sentence and found a recipe for bread pudding. It ended, "If eaten cold, serve with hot sauce. If eaten hot, serve with cold sauce." Undoubtedly she enjoyed this little set of rules for its symmetry, logic, and the fact that it sounded like a cross between Alice in Wonderland and Keats. "I eat what I see," "beauty is truth," the vice and the versa. At any rate, such specificity should certainly take care of those with "little judgment." Tucked into the same page was another of her notes, written in red ballpoint with the first word underlined and the red exclamation points engraved in the paper: "<u>Hasty</u> Pudding 2 days!!!!!" Not hasty enough, is that it? Now in her eighties, Mary Frances is working on at least two new books and several writing and editing projects. These two-day kitchen-intense recipes, these are the puddings of yesteryear.

In the chapter entitled "Some Old Fashioned Candies," her yellowed scrap directed "see Butter Scotch . . . cool." So I did. It was a recipe for molasses and sugar and butter, boiled until "it strings." It ended with the advice that "this is very nice when cooled on snow." Clearly it wasn't the making of the butterscotch that interested her. It was the cooling process. I could see her pouring the boiling butter-brown mass into a white pillow of snow. Except, of course, there is no snow in Glen Ellen, nor was there in Saint Helena, where she may well have finished off a batch of butterscotch and an article for *The New Yorker* just before her girls came home from school. Maybe she made butterscotch in snowy Switzerland, where she had a house in the thirties, before she'd had children and while she was writing her second book, *Consider the Oyster*. She probably marked this recipe because it made her remember snow and how calming it could be.

On her next marker all Mary Frances wrote was "Baked Apple Dumplings" and the page number. This she penned in a plump handwriting that befitted the recipe, or so it seemed to my eye. Anyway, I suspect she actually made these dumplings, because they were honest and un-fussy, the kind of thing she might have served to one of her thousands of luncheon guests over the years. (Maybe even to Julia Child, about whom Mary Frances had once con-fided to me, "She'll eat anything." For a moment I had found that remark perversely fascinating, bordering on the scandalous, but only for a moment. "She's not fussy, you know," she added, about her good long-time friend.)

Her feelings about the nearby "A la Mode Beef" rec-ipe were obvious from her unambiguous, empathic nota-tion: "O Poor Cook!" It wasn't a bad recipe, full of tricks and falsehoods. It was just big and boring, not her style. Whether writing an article or feeding a friend, her feelings are similar: do it from the inside out; make something of it; pay attention. It isn't spending time that bothers her; it's not getting anywhere new at the end of it. She did like something about the "To Boil a Lobster" recipe, if only the phrase she excerpted: "when the water is galloping."

When I got to the appendix—"Household Hints Old and New for Housekeepers Young and Old"—I could almost hear Mary Frances chuckling her way through. She marked the advice labeled "Save Your Old Stockings," which went thus: "Old stockings are fine for cleaning the range." Old stockings, she was probably thinking, and new stockings as well! Here at least was something practical to do with them.

Her daughters might well have been the beneficiaries, or possibly the victims, of the next two pieces of advice she noted on her papers. I tried to imagine the family scene that might have accompanied the counsel about how to soften shoes and boots: "Rub them with kerosene. Shoes will last longer, if rubbed over with drippings from roast lamb. Old-fashioned people always used mutton tallow on children's shoes." There followed this restriction on winter diets: "Do not Allow a Child to Eat Fresh Snow. This often looks clean and pure but fill a tumbler with it, cover to keep out the dust and then show it to the child, that he may see for himself, the dirt it contains."

She actually had an opportunity to perform these unnatural motions one time, when she and her daughters were stranded in a blizzard. She had described it to me in ominous tones: "No electricity. Frozen pipes, but plenty of food," she recalled, taking a deep breath, "I loved it!"

I don't know how Mary Frances resisted awarding a marker for some of the other wonderfully archaic advice, like making your own starch and "How to Lengthen the

Life of a Broom." I began to get my own ideas about what I would do with this frail book of ladylike, genteel advice. I took a sip of my tepid coffee and jotted down a few ideas quickly, then a few more. I was annoyed with myself for being so predictable, for trying to see how I might make use of these catalytic materials she had handed over with that in mind. She's always stirring things up this way, I thought, galvanizing people to take some sort of action that they ever after attribute to her influence. Nor was this dynamic limited to any one profession. It was a legacy sworn to by aerial photographers, restaurateurs who had kissed her hand only once, ecstatic poets, defoliated editors, and at least one entire religious order that ran a bakery—to name a few.

She has given me these books, I suddenly realized, but she hasn't let them go. In fact, she has given them to me so she wouldn't have to let them go. Here are my books, she was saying; now get to work. I looked at them, piled around me, her notes still transfusing their pages.

I had no way of knowing what she had originally intended for these notes of hers, whether she had used them for cooking or writing or that mysterious land within those unlikely boundaries that she has so elegantly commanded. I tried to remember something she once wrote in *The Gastronomical Me*. I walked over to my bookcase and, after a short bout with my version of alphabetical order, found my copy. One of my own scraps of paper led me to the page. "I still think that one of the pleasantest of all emotions," she had written almost a half century ago, "is to know that I, I with my brain and my hands, have nourished my beloved few, that I have concocted a stew or a story, a rarity or a plain dish, to sustain them truly against the hungers of the world."

Epilogue:

Between Friends

Whphen I started this book, M. F. K. Fisher was my friend.

I was sure of that because several years ago, while I was visiting her, she answered the phone and told the caller, much to my astonishment, "I am with my friend Jeannette."

It startled me at first. I thought maybe she just said that because she didn't know how else to put it, since I was sitting right there in front of her. Maybe what she meant was more like "I'm with my for-lack-of-a-better-term friend Jeannette."

But that's what she said, and since I liked the idea anyway, I decided to revise my interpretation of the word. The fact was that no matter how comfortable I might feel, I would never, in her presence, resort to some of my baser colloquialisms; and I always did try to wait an extra second to hear what she thought about the soup we were eating or the book we were discussing before I put my foot in it. There was no denying the undiminished respect I always felt for her or the distance that existed because of the decades of difference in our ages. I was aware, even in our giggliest times together, that she was not Suzie or Jennie or Rik. She was M. F. K. Fisher, a person without a name, never mind a nickname.

She was my friend, in very special terms.

And so I knew when I started this book that there was a delicate balance to be preserved. I wanted to portray Mary Frances as she was, as I knew her and was getting to know her, with some perspective on what she was before she invited me into her private fray. People seemed to want to think of her as a statue or a goddess or an empress; I didn't want that. I wanted to keep her alive.

The best way to do that was to take what was there, the relationship we had come up with, the friendship. She would be happy to help me, she promised; she would elaborate on anything I wished, she assured me. But I realized, right from the start, that there were many things Mary Frances did not want to discuss, areas of her life that were intimate and closed and sealed forever, as far as she was concerned. She did not have to insist on her right to privacy or dignity; it never came up.

A few times I considered resorting to a formal interview, but except for the unorganized chat we had about Brillat-Savarin, I never turned on a tape recorder in her presence. I knew that the interview technique would help to de-emphasize the personal aspect of our relationship and make it possible to discuss things. But I could never bring myself to see any value in de-emphasizing the personal aspect of our relationship. What could possibly come of it that would be better than whatever was going on? Besides, if I was going to write about the friendship, it had to be kept intact. If I became her interviewer or biographer, then everything would change. I knew about the Heisenberg principle. I had no intention of destroying the friendship in order to preserve it.

If there were things I wanted to know, I would have to poke around elsewhere, talk to bystanders and witnesses and conjecturers. Needless to say, there was a lot to ask. In the course of writing this book, I reread her books and writings and our correspondence. I traveled to Radcliffe to read her papers. I developed quite a list of questions.

There are questions about the loneliness and sorrow she experienced in the genuinely unfriendly community in which she spent her childhood. There are questions about her life in Switzerland, especially the ménage à trois, as she calls it, involving her, Al Fisher, and Dillwyn Parrish. There are questions about why her ties to the Parrish family seem to have vanished after Dillwyn's death, even though it was Dillwyn's sister Anne who sent Mary Frances's first manuscript to Harper's, her own publisher. And what of her anguish, so obliquely told, over his suicide? And what of the connection between Dillwyn's suicide and that of her brother David?

There are nothing but mysteries surrounding her life as a young widow in the early 1940s and her decision to take on the burdens of single parenthood. And what about the problems that began with her marriage to Donald Friede, the references to arrests and legal entanglements, and the upsets in his professional career that haunted their mar-

riage financially and psychologically? What of her references to being put on an FBI list?

Whatever happened to her book about childbirth?
How has she been affected by her relationship with her
daughters, one of whom has been plagued with manic de-
pression since early childhood? Why do the three of them,
who spent so many years in what would seem to be envi-
able circumstance abroad, now meet with each other so
seldom?

What happened in Piney Woods, Mississippi, where
she taught, as a volunteer, in an all-black school but was
requested not to return? What led to her final parting from
The New Yorker after years of a good relationship, which,
she once wrote to me, "I have cut . . . off, very sadly indeed
and after several decades, during which I learned a great
deal about syntax as well as manners."

Why is so much of her library devoted to works
about gypsies, witches, and sexual aberration and to mystery stories?

How does she reconcile her adamant insistence that
she reports only the truth with other people's claims that
she freely and lavishly embellishes her stories?

It takes only the smallest glint in her listener's eye to
encourage her to render a more interesting, though less
factual, version of the perils of her "flying lessons," or the
intrigues of secret societies she connived to infiltrate, or the
truth that probably lies underneath it all. "She is the maker
of her own mythology," as one Fisher admirer phrased it;
or even more to the point, as M. F. K. Fisher herself has

phrased it: "Never ruin a good story by sticking to the truth."

Perhaps the most interesting case to explore is the discrepancy in her story of her first pudding, about which she wrote in *The Gastronomical Me* in 1943 and again in *Among Friends* in 1970. Kim Chernin, in her book *The Hungry Self,* analyzes the incident, as described in *The Gastronomical Me,* calling it an important contribution to "psychological gastronomy." It is therefore especially intriguing that in the second telling, forty years later, Mary Frances revised some of the details. Since Chernin found the tale so emotionally revealing, how much more revealing it would be to compare the two versions and speculate on the meaning of the discrepancies.

Occasionally, I have tried to ask Mary Frances in a roundabout way about some of these unresolved matters. Once I picked up a handful of old photos lying in a box near her bed. I showed her a few of them and asked who the man in one of them was, hoping to generate a conversation that might encompass some of the areas of my concern. But the moment I began, she pushed them away and fell back in her bed, as if some mean person had shoved her roughly down into the sheets. "I can't do this now," she said in a faint, almost inaudible whisper that was, nevertheless, the final word.

She has other ways of stopping the action, of making you rephrase the question before you've even asked it. Her friend and agent, Robert Lescher, described it best in re-calling his first meeting with her. "She gave me that look," he said, the vision of her face still fresh in his mind. "You know the one: I am not nonplussed."

Recently I told her that Lillian Hellman's biographer, William Abrahams, had given me a piece of advice. He'd said he had so many questions about Lillian Hellman that he would give anything to be able to spend one hour with her. You must ask your questions now, he counseled, be-cause you can't trust other people's answers. Everyone lies.

"Mmmm," Mary Frances responded, wriggling away from the subject. Then she added, "Lillian Hellman lied, too, of course. . . ." And she let the matter trail off.

Indeed, she is the mistress of the ellipses, as someone once dubbed her. She knows when to stop, how to leave things unsaid, and how most poignantly and specifically to not say them. She only suggests, it would seem, though it's almost impossible to miss the point.

I once sent her a letter referring to a few unknowns she might comment on if she wished. She quickly sent back a postcard that addressed my issues with the words: "I stand ready to answer any all questions re Donald Friede or whatever." Her language itself was the answer. She was prepared, on guard; go on, charge, my friend; I stand ready. I know not what course others might have stumbled into, but as for me, I retreated.

In writing this book, I took my cues from her sister Norah, the one person Mary Frances has loved and re-spected since the day she was born. Once when Norah and

I were discussing one of these glorious mysteries, I inquired if she had ever questioned Mary Frances about it directly.

"I know she's dying for me to ask," Norah said, her lips closing tightly together in a straight line. "But I never will."

M. F. K. Fisher:

Chronology

1908 — Mary Frances Kennedy born in Albion, Mich. on July 3 to Edith Oliver Holbrook Kennedy and Rex Kennedy; their first child.

1910 — Sister Anne born.

1911 — Family moves to Whittier, Calif.; Rex Kennedy buys *The Whittier News*.

1917 — Sister Norah born.

1919 — Brother David born.

1927–29 — Attends Illinois College, Jacksonville, Ill., and Whittier College, each for one semester; takes summer courses at the University of California, Los Angeles; attends Occidental College, Calif.

1929 — Marries Alfred Young Fisher on September 5 and moves with him to Dijon, where he is doctoral student at the university.

1932 — Returns with Fisher to live in Fisher's family's summer house at Laguna Beach, Calif.; meets Dillwyn Parrish and his wife.

1934— First bylined, paid piece published, for *Westways* magazine.

1935— Returns to Occidental College, where Fisher teaches in the English Department; Dillwyn Parrish and his wife separate.

1936— Goes to Europe with Parrish and his mother as their interpreter.

1937— Divorces Fisher; marries Dillwyn Parrish, and together they move to Switzerland.

1937— *Serve It Forth* published.

1938— Dillwyn Parrish becomes seriously ill; his leg is amputated.

1939— Returns with Parrish to live at Bareacres Ranch in Hemet, Calif.

1940— Returns with Parrish to Switzerland so he can obtain medication unavailable in the U.S.

1941— *Touch and Go,* co-authored with Parrish under the single name Victori Berne, published; suicide of Parrish; *Consider the Oyster* published.

1942— *How to Cook a Wolf* published; lives in Guadalajara, Mexico, with sister Norah, brother, David, and his wife, Sarah; suicide of David.

1942–43— Works as screenwriter for Paramount Pictures, Hollywood; writes under contract for five monthly magazines

1943 — Daughter Anne born on August 15; *The Gastronomical Me* published.

1945 — Travels to New York; meets Donald Friede; marries Friede on May 19; together they move to Bareacres Ranch.

1946 — Daughter Mary ("Kennedy") born on March 12; *Here Let Us Feast: A Book of Banquets* published.

1947 — *Not Now but Now*, her only novel, published.

1949 — *An Alphabet for Gourmets* published; translation of Jean Anthelme Brillat-Savarin's *Physiology of Taste, or, Meditations on Transcendental Gastronomy* published; Henry Volkening becomes her literary agent; mother dies of heart disease; moves with two daughters to Whittier to live with father.

1951 — Divorces Donald Friede.

1953 — Rex Kennedy dies on June 2; moves with daughters Anne and Kennedy to Saint Helena, where she resides until 1970, except for two lengthy stays abroad, in France and Switzerland.

1954 — *The Art of Eating*, a compilation of all previously published books except the novels and the translation, published.

1961 — *A Cordiall Water: A Garland of Odd & Old Receipts to Assuage the Ills of Man & Beast* published.

1962 — *The Story of Wine in California* published.

1964 — Lives for six months in Piney Woods, Miss., teaching in an all-black school.

1964 — *Map of Another Town: A Memoir of Provence* published.

1965 — Travels alone to Paris; establishes friendship with Janet Flanner; sister Anne dies of cancer.

1968 — *The Cooking of Provincial France* published.

1968–69 — writes a column for *The New Yorker*, "Gastronomy Recalled."

1969 — *With Bold Knife and Fork*, a collection of *New Yorker* pieces, published.

1970 — Sells home in Saint Helena and travels with Norah to Provence, Arles, Avignon, and Marseille; moves to present home in Glen Ellen, Calif.; *Among Friends* published.

1973 — Travels with Norah to Provence and Marseille.

1976 — Travels with Norah to Aix-en-Provence.

1978 — *A Considerable Town* published; travels with Norah to Japan and Aix-en-Provence; honored by New York's Dames d'Escoffier.

1982 — *As They Were* published.

1983 — *Two Towns in Provence*, including *Map of Another Town* and *A Considerable Town*, and *Sister Age* published.

1985 — *Spirits of the Valley* and *The Standing and the Waiting* published.

1988 — *Dubious Honors* published.

1989 — *Answer in the Affirmative & The Oldest Living Man* published.

1990 — *Boss Dog* published.

1991 — *Long Ago in France* published.

1991 — Elected to the American Academy and National Institute of Arts and Letters